G000122641

SOUTHWEST DELIGHTS

❖————————————————————❖————————————————————❖

A TREASURY OF FAVORITE SOUTHWESTERN RECIPES

BY DOROTHY K. HILBURN

Designed by Camelback Group, Inc., 6625 North Scottsdale Road, Scottsdale, Arizona 85250. Telephone: 602-948-4233. Fax: 602-483-8430. Distributed by Canyonlands Publications, 4999 East Empire, Unit A, Flagstaff, Arizona 86004. For ordering information please call (800) 283-1983.

Requests for additional information should be made to The Camelback/Canyonlands Venture at the address above, or call our toll free telephone number: 1-800-284-6539.

Library of Congress Catalog Number: 94-071229
ISBN Number: 1-879924-15-3

TABLE OF CONTENTS

INTRODUCTION

Welcome to *Southwest Delights*. I have spent my entire life living in the Southwest, making it easy for me to put together a cookbook about Southwest foods. I have found writing and researching this book to be a true 'Delight'. Food is definitely the common denominator among people. Everyone I've met, through the development and research of this book, has shown such interest and enthusiasm in my project that I've come to realize that food is not just sustenance for the body but for the heart and soul as well. Cooking brings people together from all walks of life. I've received recipes from almost everyone I've come into contact with, from what were once perfect strangers, who insisted I write down their favorite recipe, to my Optometrist, who was kind enough to send me a couple of recipes she and her husband created. I've discovered that food opens doors, as well as hearts, and here in the Southwest people are more than willing to share both.

Many people don't understand what Southwest cooking is all about. Some think it's simply 'Nouvelle' Mexican, or the style in presentation. In some ways this is true, however, I believe the true Southwest style of cooking combines the old and the new. As new people relocate to our area they bring their own regional and uniquely personal styles and combine them with the flavors of Texas, New Mexico and Arizona to create a new and exciting way of cooking, the Southwest style of eating.

Southwest cooking has its roots in Mexican and Native American cooking. The Indians of historic Mexico lived on many of the same foods still prepared in Southwestern kitchens today. Wild corn was first cultivated in Mexico thousands of years ago and is still a very important crop. Foods available to the prehistoric Indians of Mexico were potatoes, avocados, turkey, chiles, peanuts, beans, sweet potatoes, squash, pumpkins, cocoa, vanilla, melons, pineapples and tomatoes. Most of the recipes in this book utilize many of these same foods.

Settled by Spaniards, New Mexico is and has always been at the forefront of Southwest cuisine. New Mexico is often known as the home of the **ristra**, a decorative, as well as useful, way of hanging chiles to dry in strands. Chiles from dried ristras can be used in sauces or ground to a powder for use in New Mexican and other Southwest dishes. Known for its art colony as well as the outstanding examples of Southwest style foods, Santa Fe is also given credit for the renewed popularity of blue cornmeal, still considered to be a ritualistic grain by Native Americans.

The Texan influence in Southwest cooking comes from the cowboys who tended the herds of cattle and cooked along the trail. Although no one is exactly sure where the first bowl of chili was created, it's commonly believed to have been the invention of a trail cook in Texas. There are chili competitions throughout the United States, and internationally, to

Previous pages: A Southwestern Thanksgiving

determine who makes the best bowl of chili. Arguments abound over whether or not beans should be included on the list of ingredients. Purists believe that only meat, onions and spices make up a "real" bowl of chili. Others, myself included, believe that the addition of other favorite foods can only made a good thing better. Fajitas and nachos are also Texan creations which are popular in restaurants across the Southwest.

Most of the original contributions to Southwest style food preparation date back to our Mexican neighbors. However, an influx of new cooks from across America and Europe are changing the face of Southwestern cooking. There are many new cooks practicing innovative techniques in food preparation and presentation who are, in turn, bringing attention internationally to the Southwestern style of cooking.

❖————————————❖————————————❖

Commonly Used Chiles

Jalapeño chiles, small, dark green or yellow chiles with a fiery flavor.

Chipotle chiles are smoked and dried Jalapeño's that have a smoky flavor and are very hot.

California chiles, also called Anaheim chiles, are long green chiles with a mild flavor. Available in cans, either whole or chopped.

Serrano chiles are very small, green, thin and very hot, usually hotter than jalapeño chiles.

Poblano chiles, also called Anchos before being dried, are large and dark green with a mild to hot flavor. Poblanos are often used to make Chile Relleno.

Chile pequin is made from tiny yellow and green peppers that, when dried and crushed, are very, very hot. Use carefully!

Tasty Tidbits

In this book we refer to chiles and chili. **Chiles** are hot peppers and **chili** is a stew-like dish.

Tomatillos: Are small, green tomato-like vegetables with an outer papery husk, if they are unavailable, use green tomatoes.

Chili powder is made up of a blend of ground chili peppers with several other seasonings.

Store **fresh chiles** in a bag in the refrigerator, or, string by the stems and hang to dry in a dry cool place.

All **squash blossoms** are edible. Zucchini blossoms are the most often used and can often be found in gourmet grocery stores in the summer.

SNACKS AND APPETIZERS
FROM QUAIL EGGS TO CACTUS

Southwestern appetizers and snacks are heavily influenced by our neighbors across the border. Many of the same foods eaten by early inhabitants of the Southwest are being prepared and presented today as appetizers or, in larger portions, as main dishes. Tortillas, tomatoes, cheeses and chiles are used to create an almost never ending selection of dishes. With a large selection fresh fruits and vegetables available for much of the year, although quail eggs can be hard to come by, Southwest cooks have the many fresh ingredients necessary to prepare historical Southwestern recipes or to create their own new recipes.

❖ ———————————————— ❖ ———————————————— ❖

CAMEMBERT QUESADILLA

The full flavor of Camembert cheese makes this Quesadilla an extra tasty appetizer. Serve with your favorite salsa and a dollop of sour cream.

INGREDIENTS:

10 flour tortillas
1 teaspoon butter
1 pound Camembert cheese, cut into strips

2 poblano chiles, roasted, peeled and chopped
1 small onion, sliced thin

Sauté onion slices in butter until tender. Heat flour tortillas by placing in a large hot pan and heating each side for 10 to 15 seconds. Place the Camembert strips, onion slices and chopped chiles on 1/2 of a flour tortilla and fold. Heat quesadilla until the cheese melts then cut into triangular wedges. Place in a warm oven until all tortillas have been filled.

❖ ———————————————— ❖ ———————————————— ❖

SAVORY SOUTHWEST SALMON DIP

This tasty dip can be served with crackers and veggies or as a spread.

INGREDIENTS:

1 cup flaked canned salmon
8 ounces cottage cheese
4 slices cooked bacon, diced

1/4 cup pickle relish
1/3 cup sour cream

In a medium mixing bowl, combine salmon, cottage cheese, bacon, relish and sour cream. Mix well and chill before serving.

Potato Omelette, Shrimp Kabobs and Scallops.

TUNA AND CHILE DIP

This makes a cool, tasty dip that can also be used as a sandwich spread. I have trouble deciding which way I prefer it myself!

INGREDIENTS:

1 7 ounce can tuna, drained
1 tablespoon olive oil
1/2 cup onion, chopped
1/4 cup jalapeño pepper, chopped
1/4 cup scallions, chopped
1/2 cup capers, drained

1/3 cup celery, chopped
1 medium tomato, chopped
2 tablespoons lime juice
1/4 teaspoon seasoned salt
1/2 bag tortilla chips
1/4 cup cheese, grated

Combine drained tuna, olive oil, onion, jalapeño pepper, scallions, capers, celery, tomato, lime juice and seasoned salt in a large bowl. Toss to mix well. Garnish with grated cheese and serve with tortilla chips.

DEE LINDA'S CON QUESO

My sister, Dee Linda, makes this cheese dip whenever she entertains. People come to her parties to enjoy her graciousness and her dip!

INGREDIENTS:

1 2 lb package Velveeta cheese,
cut into large chunks
1 bunch scallions, chopped
6 medium tomatoes, chopped

1 7 3/4 ounce can El Pato tomato
sauce (Mexican hot style)
1 bag tortilla chips

In a crock pot, combine Velveeta, scallions, tomatoes and chile sauce. Cook on high heat until cheese melts. When cheese has melted lower heat and serve with tortilla chips.

GUACAMOLE

Guacamole, used as a dip or an edible garnish, is always popular.

INGREDIENTS:

4 avocados, mashed
2 tomatoes, diced
2 green onions, diced

1 pint sour cream
1 4 ounce can green chiles, diced
Salt

Mix avocados, tomatoes and onions with sour cream. Add green chiles and salt to taste. Serve with tortilla chips.

SWEET PEPPER BALLS

These fabulous appetizers take a little time to make, but they are worth the effort. Prepare ahead and freeze to save time on party day.

INGREDIENTS:

2 pounds beef, boiled
2 pounds pork, boiled
2 7 ounce cans green chiles, drained and chopped
1 large sweet onion, diced
2 large eggs

1/2 cup sugar
1/2 cup raisins
1/2 cup walnuts, chopped fine
1/2 cup flour
2/3 cup shortening

Boil meat until cooked thoroughly. Put the cooled meat through a meat grinder. Cook onions and add the ground meat, chiles, sugar, raisins and walnuts and stir to mix well. Set aside to cool. Separate egg whites and yolks. Beat whites until they become quite stiff then fold in beaten yolks. Place in a shallow dish. Place a small amount of flour in one hand and shape meat mixture into small balls, about the size of a small egg. Roll each ball in the egg mixture then place in very hot oil. Using a slotted spoon, turn each ball until lightly brown all over. Place on paper towels to drain excess oils and serve. Makes approximately 4 dozen.

CHEESE CRISP

These cheese crisps are a simple but filling snack. Serve with a favorite salsa, sour cream, a dash of Tabasco sauce and guacamole on the side to make a light meal.

INGREDIENTS:

1 large flour tortilla
1 tablespoon crushed red peppers

1/2 cup Cheddar cheese, grated

Place tortilla on a flat baking sheet and sprinkle cheese evenly over the top. Bake under medium heat, about 350°F, until cheese is completely melted. Sprinkle with crushed red peppers. Serves 2.

Green Chile Dip

Avocados and chiles combined create a creamy and flavorful dip sure to be a favorite at any gathering.

INGREDIENTS:

1 4 oz can green chiles, drained and chopped
1 avocado, diced

1 cup sour cream
1/2 teaspoon salt
1/2 teaspoon Tabasco sauce

Mix chiles, avocado, salt and Tabasco sauce in sour cream. Chill for an hour and serve with tortilla chips or celery sticks. Serves 8.

Stuffed Mushrooms

This sophisticated appetizer is a staple at many parties and is appreciated by mushroom lovers everywhere.

INGREDIENTS:

1 medium onion, minced
1 clove garlic, minced
2 pounds mushrooms, minced
40 large mushroom caps

4 tablespoons butter
1 1/2 cups breadcrumbs
1 cup Romano cheese, grated
Salt and pepper

Preheat oven to 450°F. In a medium pan, sauté onion, garlic and minced mushrooms in butter. Combine breadcrumbs, Romano cheese and salt and pepper to taste. Let cool. Rinse mushroom caps and let dry. Fill mushrooms with onion mixture then top with the Romano cheese and breadcrumbs. Bake for 10 minutes and serve warm. Makes 40.

Nachos

INGREDIENTS:

1 package tortilla chips
1/2 cup sliced jalapeño chiles

1/2 lb Monterey cheese, grated
1/2 lb Cheddar cheese, grated

On a large baking sheet place a layer of tortilla chips, covering the pan completely. Spread shredded cheese and sliced jalapeño chiles over corn chips and add another layer of chips. Spread cheese and chiles over top and place under broiler until cheese melts.

Corn Chips with Chili Jelly

BOILED EGGS STUFFED WITH SALMON

An elegant and unusual tasting finger food, this recipe has been passed around and enjoyed by many of my closest friends.

INGREDIENTS:

6 hard boiled eggs
2 ounces salmon, steamed, boned and flaked
4 tablespoons tomato sauce
1 tablespoon minced pimento
1/4 tablespoon Worcestershire sauce
1 tablespoon minced fresh onion

2 1/2 tablespoons minced dill pickle
1/4 teaspoon pickle juice
1/8 teaspoon cayenne pepper
2 tablespoons minced Spanish olives
Salt and pepper

Cut eggs lengthwise and remove yolks. Discard all but 3 of the egg yolks. In a mixing bowl, combine salmon, tomato sauce, minced pimento, Worcestershire sauce, minced onion, minced pickle, pickle juice, cayenne powder, and salt and pepper to taste. Fill egg whites with mixture and garnish with minced Spanish olives. Refrigerate until ready to serve.

❖————————————❖————————————❖

SCALLOP CEVICHE

INGREDIENTS:

1/2 pound scallops
Juice from 1 lemon
Juice from 1 lime
1/4 red onion, minced
1 plum tomato, diced
1 jalapeño pepper, minced
1 serrano chile pepper, minced

1/2 cup cilantro, chopped
1 green onion, chopped
1 teaspoon ketchup
1/2 teaspoon rice wine vinegar
1/8 teaspoon cayenne pepper
1/8 teaspoon pepper
Salt

Combine scallops, lemon and lime juice, red onion, plum tomato, jalapeño pepper, serrano chile pepper, cilantro, green onion, ketchup, rice wine vinegar, cayenne pepper, black pepper and salt to taste. Mix well and refrigerate for at least 4 hours, or overnight. Serves 5.

❖————————————❖————————————❖

A WORD ABOUT SNACKS:

To make interesting new flavors of popcorn that are low in fat and high in flavor, sprinkle chili powder, brewers yeast or cayenne pepper over freshly popped corn.

POTATO OMELET

This is a traditional Spanish dish that is served as *Tapas* (a spicy finger food). Serve with, or without, a sauce on the side.

INGREDIENTS:

4 large potatoes, peeled and sliced very thin
4 eggs
1 large onion, sliced thin

1 cup olive oil
1 tablespoon parsley, chopped
2 tablespoons chopped pimentos
Salt and pepper

Preheat oven to 325°F. Using a non-stick skillet, heat the oil and add potatoes, one slice at a time. After each layer of potatoes add a layer of onions and salt and pepper. Cook over low heat, turning the potatoes often, do not allow to brown. Place cooked potatoes in a colander to drain oil. Reserve 3 tablespoons of oil. In a large bowl, beat eggs until foamy and add salt, parsley, pimentos and potatoes. Make sure potatoes are covered by the egg mixture. Set mixture aside to soak for 15 minutes. In a non-stick, oven-proof skillet, heat reserved oil. When the oil begins to smoke, add the potato mixture, spreading evenly over the bottom of the pan. Lower heat and continue to cook for 4 more minutes. Transfer the skillet to the oven and cook for 20 minutes, or until the top becomes a golden brown. Omelet should be firm to the touch. Place omelet on a platter and let cool. Cut into slices and serve at room temperature.

DEVILED SHRIMP

This zesty flavored appetizer is a guaranteed hit at any party. Make the day before your event to give you more time for other preparations.

INGREDIENTS:

1/2 cup dry white wine
1/2 cup wine vinegar
2 tablespoons mustard
1 teaspoon horseradish
1/2 tablespoon paprika
1/2 teaspoon cayenne pepper

2 tablespoons ketchup
1/4 teaspoon garlic powder
1 cup vegetable oil
1 pound cooked shrimp
1/2 teaspoon salt
1 red or yellow bell pepper, sliced

In a large mixing bowl, combine white wine, vinegar, ketchup, mustard, horseradish, garlic powder, cayenne pepper, paprika, oil and salt. Beat ingredients until blended well. Add shrimp to marinade and let sit for at least 3 hours in refrigerator. Drain shrimp and serve with pepper slices. Serves 6.

CHILES, SALSAS AND SAUCES
FROM SALSA TO PESTO

Chiles are one of the most important and most often used ingredients in Southwest cooking. The many different varieties of chiles, each having its own distinctive flavor, add an important taste and texture to our way of cooking. The flavors of chiles vary as much as their shapes and sizes. A common misconception about chiles is their heat. Not all chiles are fiery hot, many are actually very mild. The hottest part of the chile is the interior vein which houses a substance called capsaicin. Seeds and the placenta are also very hot due to their close proximity to the capsaicin. Since all chiles have their own flavor, even chiles grown on the same plant may have different tastes, the only way to really know how hot a chile may be is to taste it. A word of caution, chiles can be very addictive, once you start eating them you may never want to stop!

❖ ———————————— ❖ ———————————— ❖

PREPARATION OF CHILES

Preparing fresh chiles is quite easy. Wear rubber gloves when handling chiles and, most importantly, make sure your hands do not come into contact with your eyes, nose or mouth. The eyes are especially sensitive to chile oils. Wash chiles and dry well. Char the skin of the chiles over a gas stove, barbecue, under a broiler, or in a heavy skillet. Turn often to blacken the skins evenly and to prevent the flesh of the chiles from burning. When the chiles' skins are black and blistered, place chiles in a plastic or brown paper bag for 10 minutes. This allows the steam to loosen the skins from the chiles. Charring the skins gives the chiles a very nice smokey flavor. Wearing rubber gloves, peel off loosened skin. If you are planning to use the chiles whole, slit the side of the chile and remove seeds and stem. Rinse chiles in cold water. Chiles can be frozen with or without the skin and will last several months in the freezer.

❖ ———————————— ❖ ———————————— ❖

FRESH SALSA

This delicious salsa is wonderful when accompanying any meal.

INGREDIENTS:

3 large tomatoes, diced
1/2 cup cilantro, chopped
1 medium onion, chopped

4 tablespoons lemon juice
1/4 cup jalapeño chiles, chopped
Salt and pepper

Mix tomatoes, cilantro, onion, lemon juice, and chiles together. Salt and pepper to taste. Chill before serving. Makes 3 cups.

Fresh Salsa

RED CHILE SALSA

This colorful and versatile sauce can be used as a simple salsa served with tortilla chips or served over pasta.

INGREDIENTS:

5 dried poblano chiles
1 cup boiling water
1 teaspoon red chili pepper, crushed
1 cup Italian plum tomatoes, drained and chopped
1 onion, chopped

1/8 teaspoon garlic powder
1/4 cup olive oil
1 teaspoon sugar
1/2 teaspoon salt
1/4 teaspoon pepper
1 tablespoon lemon juice

Chop poblano chiles, removing stem and seeds. Place chiles in boiling water and let sit for 1/2 hour. Drain, and reserve, chile water. Mix chiles, 1/4 cup chile water, crushed red chili peppers, onion, tomatoes and garlic powder. Purée mixture in a blender until smooth. In a small pan, heat olive oil and add purée. Add the sugar, salt and pepper and cook for 5 minutes. Remove from heat and let sit for 15 minutes. Add lemon juice and mix well. Serve warm. Makes 2 cups.

❖─────────────────❖─────────────────❖

GAZPACHO RELISH

This cool relish goes well with grilled meats, as a salsa, or with almost any omelet. Let your taste buds decide which is best!

INGREDIENTS:

3 large tomatoes
1/4 cup onion, diced
1/2 cup green pepper, diced
1/3 cup vinegar
3/4 teaspoon celery salt

3/4 teaspoon mustard seed
1/4 teaspoon salt
1/4 teaspoon pepper
1 tablespoon sugar

Peel and dice tomatoes. Place tomatoes, pepper and onion in a medium mixing bowl. In a small mixing bowl, combine vinegar, celery salt, mustard seed, salt, pepper and sugar. Mix well before pouring over tomato mixture. Mix to blend. Chill for 2 to 3 hours. Makes 3 cups.

❖─────────────────❖─────────────────❖

PESTO SAUCE

INGREDIENTS:

1 cup fresh basil, firmly packed
1/2 cup fresh parsley
1/2 cup Parmesan cheese, grated
1/4 cup pine nuts

2 cloves garlic, quartered
1/3 cup olive oil
Salt

Place basil, parsley, Parmesan cheese, pine nuts, garlic and 1/4 teaspoon salt in a blender. Blend until a paste forms then add oil, 1 tablespoon at a time, while blending. When paste becomes soft and creamy, pesto is finished. Refrigerate or freeze. Heat pesto before using and use with pasta or meats. Makes 2 cups.

TOMATO AND CHILI SAUCE

This basic tomato based sauce is versatile enough to be spread over anything from enchiladas to pasta. The chili powder gives it an extra boost of flavor. Prepare ahead and freeze.

INGREDIENTS:

1/2 cup onion, minced
3 cups tomato purée
1/2 teaspoon garlic powder
3 tablespoons chili powder
2 tablespoons olive oil

1/2 teaspoon basil
1/2 teaspoon oregano
1/8 teaspoon cumin
Salt
Pepper

Saute onion in oil until tender. Add tomato purée, garlic, chili powder, basil, oregano and cumin. Stir to mix well and simmer for 1 hour. Strain mixture. Salt and pepper to taste. Serve over chicken, enchiladas or anything tomato sauce is used for. Makes 4 cups.

CHILI VINEGAR

This vinegar can be combined with olive oil and other ingredients to make dressings and marinades sure to add extra flavor to many foods.

INGREDIENTS:

12 chiles, red or green, charred and seeded

6 cups white distilled vinegar

Quarter prepared chiles before bringing vinegar to a boil. Add chiles and boil mixture for 3 minutes. Set aside to cool slightly and pour chiles and vinegar into a large jar. Cover tightly and let sit for 6 weeks. Strain the mixture into 3 or 4 smaller jars and cover tightly.

CHILI SAUCE

This tasty chili sauce can be used to baste beef or chicken before grilling. If you're still a tender foot when it comes to chili, use less chili powder.

INGREDIENTS:

1 medium onion, chopped
4 tablespoons olive oil
2 cloves garlic, chopped fine
3 cups chicken broth
1/3 cup tomato purée
1 tablespoon wine vinegar

1/4 teaspoon cayenne pepper
1/4 teaspoon oregano
5 tablespoons chili powder
1 1/2 teaspoons cornstarch
Salt and pepper to taste

Sauté onion and garlic in olive oil until tender. Add broth, tomato purée, oregano, vinegar and cayenne pepper. Mix chili powder with water to make a paste and add to sauce. Stir mixture thoroughly. Simmer for 45 minutes. Strain mixture and return to pan. Salt and pepper to taste. Mix cornstarch with a small amount of water before adding to chili mixture. Simmer, stirring often until sauce thickens. Makes 3 cups.

CHILI BUTTER

INGREDIENTS:

1/2 pound butter	1 teaspoon garlic powder
1 teaspoon chili powder	2 tablespoons lemon juice

When butter is room temperature, add salt, chili powder, garlic powder and lemon juice. Mix well and chill. Refrigerate after using.

❖ ———————————— ❖ ———————————— ❖

A WORD ABOUT CHILES:

The heat of a chile comes from the capsaicin oil which is concentrated in the placenta, or veins, of the chile. The seeds are hot because of their close proximity to the veins. The Anaheim chile, also called California chile, is a large, mild flavored green or yellow chile. Jalapeño chiles are small, green or yellow and so hot you may think your mouth is on fire. When a Jalapeño chile has been smoked and dried it becomes a Chipotle chile. Chipotle chiles have a wonderful smoky flavor.

WESTERN SWEET RELISH

Using fresh ingredients is always best, however, canned substitutions will do nicely if fresh ingredients are unavailable.

INGREDIENTS:

1 head cabbage, diced
2 white onions, diced
2 sweet green peppers, diced
2 sweet red peppers, diced
4 1/2 tablespoons mustard seed

2 teaspoons celery seed
1 quart vinegar
4 cups sugar
3 hot peppers, crushed
5 tablespoons salt

Combine diced cabbage, onions, green peppers and red peppers in a large bowl. In another mixing bowl, combine mustard seed, celery seed, vinegar, sugar, crushed hot peppers and salt. Stir until sugar dissolves then pour over diced vegetables. Toss well and refrigerate over night. Spoon mixture into jars and seal tightly. Let sit for 2 days. Makes 4 quarts.

❖————————————————❖————————————————❖

CHILI JELLY

A special Southwestern treat, serve with a block of cream cheese and pepper crackers or as a side with pork.

INGREDIENTS:

4 red chile pods, dried
4 sweet green peppers, peeled and seeded

5 3/4 cups sugar
1 cup vinegar
1 box Sure-jell

Rinse the dried chile pods and remove the stem and seeds. In a blender, grind chile and green peppers. Add sugar and vinegar and boil until mixture is clear. Let cool for 5 minutes. Add Sure-jell and stir. Place mixture into small jars and seal. Refrigerate after opening.

❖————————————————❖————————————————❖

ROASTED PIÑON NUTS

INGREDIENTS:

1 pound raw piñon (pine) nuts

Preheat oven to 300°F. Spread nuts evenly in a shallow baking pan and roast for 1 hour, stirring often to brown evenly.

CHIPOTLE SAUCE

Chipotle sauce is often served over chicken and pork dishes.

INGREDIENTS:

1 to 3 chipotle chiles, chopped
1 15 ounce can tomato sauce
2 medium tomatoes, chopped
1 clove garlic, pressed

1 medium onion, chopped
2 tablespoons vegetable oil
Salt
Pepper

Sauté onion in oil and add chipotle chiles, tomato sauce, chopped tomatoes, garlic and salt and pepper to taste. Cook over medium heat for 20 minutes. Makes 1 quart.

❖―――――――――❖―――――――――❖

FRESH FRUIT SALSA

If you don't have these fruits handy, improvise by using pineapple, watermelon or even an avocado. Serve on an attractive dish.

INGREDIENTS:

1 papaya, diced
1 cucumber, diced
1 cup strawberries, cleaned and diced

1 cantaloupe, peeled and diced
3 tablespoons lime juice
3 tablespoons honey

Combine lime juice and honey. In a large bowl, combine diced papaya, cucumber, strawberries and cantaloupe. Pour honey-lime mixture over fruit and chill for 1 hour before serving.

❖―――――――――❖―――――――――❖

CUCUMBER DRESSING

INGREDIENTS:

1 large cucumber
3 cloves garlic, pressed
2 tablespoons fresh dill, diced
1 teaspoon jalapeño chili, diced

2 tablespoons lemon juice
1 cup nonfat yogurt
2 tablespoons olive oil
Salt and pepper

Peel, seed and dice the cucumber. In a blender, combine cucumber, garlic, dill and jalapeño pepper. Blend until smooth. In a medium mixing bowl, pour cucumber mixture and fold in lemon juice, yogurt, olive oil and salt and pepper to taste. Refrigerate before serving. Makes 2 cups.

SOUPS AND SALADS
FROM HOT TO COLD

Maybe it's the weather, or the simple and easy lifestyle here in the Southwest, that has made soups and salads a mainstay of our diets. With the availability of a wide variety of fresh fruits and vegetables we are able to create simple, healthy and tasty salads and soups, both hot and cold. As always, I urge you to experiment with your favorite foods to create your own traditions, wherever you may live.

TORTILLA SOUP

The simple ingredients used in this recipe come together to make this one of my favorite soups. Tortilla soup can be found on the menus of many restaurants across the Southwest.

INGREDIENTS:

2 quarts chicken or beef stock
1/2 cup onion, chopped
1 clove garlic, minced
1 cup tomato sauce
1/2 teaspoon salt

1/4 teaspoon pepper
6 or 8 stale tortillas
1 1/2 cups Monterey Jack cheese, shredded
Oil for frying

Heat stock, with onion and garlic, to boiling. Simmer for 5 minutes. Add tomato sauce, salt and pepper and simmer for 5 minutes. Cut tortillas into strips and fry in hot oil until they become crisp. Spoon soup over a handful of tortilla strips to serve. Garnish with grated cheese.

CORN SOUP

Corn Soup was first cooked by Southwestern Native Americans before the birth of Christ and is still popular today.

INGREDIENTS:

4 cups fresh corn
1 cup chicken stock
1/4 cup butter
4 cups milk

1/2 cup green onion, chopped
6 tablespoons sour cream
3 tablespoons green chiles, diced
Salt and pepper

Blend corn and chicken stock to smooth purée. Sauté green onions in butter until tender. Add corn purée and cook over medium heat for about 8 minutes, or until thickened. Add milk and salt and pepper to taste and cook for 10 minutes. Garnish with sour cream and chiles.

BELL PEPPER SOUP

This colorful and oh-so-savory soup is an instant favorite for anyone lucky enough to taste it. Make some for your loved ones.

INGREDIENTS:

3 red bell peppers, roasted, peeled and seeded
1 1/2 cups chicken stock
2 medium carrots, chopped
1/2 onion, chopped

1/4 cup celery, chopped
1/3 teaspoon cayenne pepper
1 cup whipping cream
Salt

In a medium saucepan, combine bell peppers, chicken stock, carrots, onion, celery and cayenne pepper. Bring to a boil. Simmer over medium low for 10 minutes. Transfer to a food processor and purée. Add salt to taste. Return to saucepan and add cream. Simmer until mixture thickens.

❖————————————————❖————————————————❖

CUCUMBER SALAD

This cool, zesty salad is an excellent side dish and goes well with grilled meats. For extra color, garnish with mandarin orange slices.

INGREDIENTS:

3 large cucumbers
1/3 cup vinegar
2 tablespoons water
1/4 cup sugar

1 teaspoon salt
1/4 teaspoon ground pepper
1 tablespoon minced dill

Peel cucumbers and slice very thin. Refrigerate slices in a bowl of ice water for at least 1 hour. In a small mixing bowl, combine vinegar, water, sugar, and salt and pepper. Drain cucumbers and pat dry. Place slices in a bowl and pour vinegar mixture over top. Refrigerate for 1 hour. Garnish with dill before serving. Serves 6.

❖————————————————❖————————————————❖

CHILI AND AVOCADO SOUP

INGREDIENTS:

2 large avocados
2 cups chicken broth
1 1/2 cups half and half

1/4 teaspoon chili powder
Salt
Pepper

Peel and pit avocados and mash. Place mashed avocados and chicken broth in a medium pan and simmer for 10 minutes, stirring often. Remove from heat and add half and half, chili powder and salt and pepper to taste. Stir to mix well and refrigerate, covered, for 1 hour. Serves 4.

❖————————————❖————————————❖

PUMPKIN SOUP

A wonderful way to celebrate the change of seasons. Even here in the Southwest we enjoy traditional fall favorites. Good served cold, too.

INGREDIENTS:

1 cup canned pumpkin
3 1/2 cups milk
2 tablespoons butter
1/2 teaspoon sugar

1/8 teaspoon nutmeg (optional)
Salt
Pepper
1/4 cup sunflower seeds

In a medium sauce pan bring milk to a boil and add pumpkin. Stir in butter, sugar, nutmeg (if used) and salt and pepper. Simmer over very low heat for 5 to 10 minutes. Garnish with sunflower seeds. Serves 4.

❖————————————❖————————————❖

CHILI CON QUESO SOUP

INGREDIENTS:

1/2 pound lean ground beef
1 medium potato, chopped fine
1 medium onion, chopped fine
2 green chiles, peeled, seeded
and diced
2 medium tomatoes, chopped fine
1 1/2 teaspoon chili powder
2 cloves garlic, minced
1 teaspoon oregano

1/2 teaspoon cumin
1 teaspoon salt
1/3 cup flour
4 chicken bouillon cubes
2 quarts hot water
1/3 cup cold water
Tortilla chips
3/4 cup Cheddar cheese, shredded

In a large pot, cook ground beef, potato, onion, chiles, tomatoes, chili powder, garlic, oregano, cumin and salt. Add bouillon cubes to the hot water and stir until dissolved then add to ground beef mixture. Simmer for 15 minutes. In a separate bowl, mix cold water and flour. Pour slowly into soup, stirring constantly. Simmer for 15 minutes, or until desired thickness is reached. Garnish with tortilla chips and cheese. Serves 8.

SOUTHWEST TOMATO SOUP

This is not your everyday tomato soup recipe. Jalapeño peppers give this easy to prepare soup it's special flavor.

INGREDIENTS:

3 cups tomato juice
1 6 ounce can tomato paste
1 onion, diced
2 slices bacon, chopped

1/8 teaspoon baking soda
1 cup half and half
1 jalapeño pepper, diced
Salt and pepper

In a medium saucepan, cook bacon and onion until onion becomes tender. Add tomato juice, tomato paste, baking soda and salt and pepper to taste. Simmer over very low heat for 10 minutes then add half and half. Stir and cook until soup just becomes hot, do not bring soup to a boil. Garnish with diced jalapeño pepper. Serves 6.

CHILI POBLANO SOUP

This hearty soup is a substantial meal all by itself. I serve it with chile-corn bread and cold Mexican beer.

INGREDIENTS:

1/4 pound lean pork, cubed
1 small onion, chopped
1 cup corn, fresh from the cob or frozen
1 poblano chile, sliced
1 zucchini, sliced

3 tablespoons tomato purée
1 quart chicken stock
1 avocado, sliced
1/2 cup Monterey Jack cheese, shredded
Salt and pepper

Brown pork cubes in a medium pan. Add the onion, corn, poblano chile, zucchini, tomato purée and chicken stock. Add salt and pepper to taste and simmer for 20 minutes. Garnish soup with avocado slices and shredded cheese. Serves 4.

A WORD ABOUT SOUP STOCK:

Homemade soup stock is far and away the best when preparing soups. Save chicken or beef parts and when you have enough, simmer chicken or beef parts in 4 quarts of water. Add an onion, a clove of garlic and salt and pepper to taste. Simmer for 2 hours. When cool, skim fat. Strain and freeze for future use.

COLD APPLE SOUP

A cool and refreshing dish to serve as a first course. Apple soup is an excellent starter to grilled pork or chicken.

INGREDIENTS:

4 1/2 Granny Smith apples	1/4 cup sour cream
1 cup dry white wine	1 cup beef stock
2 cinnamon sticks	1 cup heavy cream
2 slices fresh ginger	1/2 teaspoon salt
5 tablespoons sugar	Juice from 1 lemon
1 tablespoon apple brandy	

Peel, core and cut 4 apples into quarters. Take the half apple and dice well. Sprinkle diced apple with lemon juice and set aside. In a large saucepan, combine quartered apples, wine, cinnamon sticks, ginger and sugar. Bring to a boil before covering and reduce heat. Cook over medium heat for 10 minutes. Cool and discard cinnamon sticks and ginger. Place remaining mixture, apples included, into a blender with the apple brandy and sour cream. Blend until smooth then add stock and cream, while the blender is running. Add remaining lemon juice and salt, again while the blender is still running. Chill, garnish with diced apples before serving.

CHILE AND BEAN SALAD

A cool salad, just the right thing for those hot summer nights. Serve with gazpacho soup and a cool dessert.

INGREDIENTS:

1 large bell pepper, seeded	2 scallions, sliced thin
1 16 oz can black beans, drained	4 teaspoons lemon juice
1 large tomato, diced	3 teaspoons olive oil
2 jalapeño peppers, seeded and diced	Salt
	Pepper

Combine olive oil, lemon juice, jalapeño peppers and salt and pepper to taste, set aside. In a salad bowl, combine bell pepper, black beans, tomato, and scallions. Pour dressing over all and toss well. Refrigerate before serving. Serves 4.

A WORD ABOUT SPICES:

Paprika, made from dried red bell peppers, is high in vitamins A and C.

TOMATILLO SALAD

Tomatillos are small, tomato-like vegetables with a papery outer husk. Though similar to tomatoes, they have a unique flavor all their own.

INGREDIENTS:

6 tomatillos
1/4 cup olive oil
2 tablespoons lime juice

1 teaspoon pepper
3/4 cup Parmesan cheese, grated
1/2 cup piñon nuts

Husk tomatillos and rinse thoroughly. Thinly slice tomatillos and place on salad plates. Mix olive oil and lime juice and pepper and pour a small amount over each plate of tomatillo slices. Garnish with Parmesan cheese and piñon nuts. Serves 4.

GAZPACHO SOUP

A classic Mexican soup that has become very popular in the Southwest. Garnish with avocados and croutons.

INGREDIENTS:

8 to 10 tomatoes, chopped
2 cups tomato juice
1 cucumber, diced
1/4 cup cilantro, chopped
2 tablespoons parsley, minced
2 cloves garlic, minced
1 jalapeño pepper, chopped

2 tablespoons wine vinegar
2 tablespoons lime juice
1 teaspoon olive oil
1 avocado, diced
2 cups croutons
Salt
Pepper

Blend 1/2 of the tomatoes, 1 cup tomato juice, cucumber, cilantro, garlic, jalapeño pepper, wine vinegar, lime juice, parsley and olive oil in a blender until almost smooth. Add the remaining tomatoes and tomato juice and refrigerate overnight to allow flavors to blend. Serve in chilled bowls and garnish with diced avocados and croutons. Serves 4.

RICH RICE AND NUT SALAD

You will love this wonderfully flavored rice salad. Serve with a loaf of crusty french bread and a glass of wine.

INGREDIENTS:

1 1/2 cups cooked brown rice
2 tablespoons olive oil
2 tablespoons lemon juice
1/4 cucumber, chopped
5 black olives, pitted and chopped
1/2 cup cashews, chopped
1/2 cup walnuts, chopped

1/2 cup blanched almonds, chopped
1/2 cup golden raisins
1/4 cup currants
1 15 ounce can peach slices
Salt
Pepper

Combine olive oil, lemon juice and salt and pepper to taste. Mix well and set aside. Soak dried fruits, drain. In a large bowl, combine cooked rice, cucumbers, black olives, nuts, softened fruit, and peaches. Shake dressing well and pour over salad, toss well. Serve on a bed of lettuce. Serves 4.

❖ ———————————————— ❖ ———————————————— ❖

BLACK BEAN SOUP

INGREDIENTS:

1 pound dried black beans, washed thoroughly
2 quarts boiling water
2 tablespoons salt
1/8 teaspoon garlic powder
1 1/2 teaspoons cumin

1 1/2 teaspoons oregano
2 tablespoons white vinegar
10 tablespoons olive oil
2 onions, peeled and chopped
2 green peppers, chopped

Cook beans in boiling water for 2 minutes. Cover and remove from heat. Let sit for 1 hour. Add salt and resume cooking. Simmer for 2 hours, until beans are soft. In a blender, place garlic, cumin, oregano and vinegar and blend until it becomes a thick paste. Sauté onions and green peppers in olive oil until tender. Add onions, green peppers and garlic mixture to beans. Simmer over low heat until ready to serve. Serves 6.

❖ ———————————————— ❖ ———————————————— ❖

GARLIC CROUTONS

INGREDIENTS:

1 loaf stale bread
1/2 cup butter
1/4 cup olive oil

3/4 teaspoon garlic powder
2 tablespoons parsley
Salt and pepper

Cut bread into 1 inch cubes and spread evenly over baking sheet. Let dry completely. In a large skillet, heat butter and oil and add garlic, parsley, and salt and pepper to taste. Place bread cubes into a large bowl and pour butter mixture over croutons. Fry to a light brown.

Following Pages: Prickly Pear Salad

SPINACH SALAD

An extremely healthy salad that can be adapted to your own tastes. Serve with your favorite dressing or try my poppy seed recipe below.

INGREDIENTS FOR SALAD:

2 bunches of spinach, trimmed and cleaned

2 bunches of watercress

INGREDIENTS FOR POPPY SEED DRESSING:

1/2 cup sugar
1 teaspoon salt
1 teaspoon dry mustard
1/2 teaspoon onion powder

1/3 cup white balsamic vinegar
1 cup oil
1 tablespoon lime juice
1 1/2 tablespoons poppy seed

Mix sugar, salt, mustard, onion powder, white balsamic vinegar, and lime juice. Stir to dissolve sugar. Stir in oil slowly, beating well. Add poppy seeds. Chill before pouring over mixed greens. Serves 4.

SPICY VINEGAR

INGREDIENTS:

1 quart white vinegar
2 teaspoons peppercorns
1 teaspoon whole allspice

1 teaspoon mustard seed
2 blades of mace
1 stick of cinnamon

Tie all spices in a cheesecloth and combine with vinegar in an enamel or stainless steel pan. Cover and bring to a boil. Remove from heat as soon as the mixture begins to boil and let steep for 2 hours. Remove bag and store in sterilized, attractive bottles.

APRICOT VINEGAR

INGREDIENTS:

1 cup dried apricots

1 quart red wine vinegar

In a stainless steel pan, warm vinegar before pouring over apricots that have been placed in a sterilized jar. Seal tightly, let sit for 4 to 6 weeks. Remove apricots before using. Keep in a sterilized jar or bottle.

ZUCCHINI SOUP

This distinctive soup can be served hot or cold. Serve as a starter with with your choice of a grilled chicken or fish dish.

INGREDIENTS:

4 large zucchini
2 cups water
1 cup chicken broth
2 tablespoons parsley leaves
2 tablespoons butter

1 13 ounce can evaporated milk
1 tablespoon onion, diced
1 tablespoon flour
Parsley
Salt and pepper

Cut zucchini into large pieces, make sure to wash and cut stems first. Place zucchini and water in a pot and bring to a boil. Cover pot and let simmer for 15 minutes. Remove from heat and let cool. Strain zucchini, reserving 1 cup cooking liquid, and place in a blender. Add 2 tablespoons parsley and 1 cup of the cooking liquid and purée. Sauté onion in butter until tender. Add flour, cook for 1 minute, stirring. Add puréed zucchini, evaporated milk, chicken broth and salt. Cook over medium heat, stirring often, until soup comes to a boil. Garnish with parsley leaves. Serves 6.

❖ ——————————————— ❖ ——————————————— ❖

CLAM SOUP

INGREDIENTS:

2 cans clams, with juice
1 medium onion, diced
1 clove garlic
4 tablespoons olive oil

1/2 cup tomato sauce
1 sprig parsley, minced
Salt
Pepper

Sauté onion in oil and add parsley, tomato sauce and garlic. Add clams and juice and salt and pepper to taste. Heat thoroughly. Serves 4.

❖ ——————————————— ❖ ——————————————— ❖

A WORD ABOUT ARTICHOKES:

When buying fresh artichokes, look for a solid head of about 3 to 3 1/2 inches in diameter. Avoid the larger artichokes because they tend to be too fibrous. Check the outside and avoid artichokes with brown, cracked or withered stems or leaves, this shows age. Fresh artichokes, stored in a closed bags in the refrigerator, will last 2 to 3 days.

COLESLAW

There are so many different coleslaw recipes I could only choose my favorite. Add some diced red pepper to create a Southwest version.

INGREDIENTS:

1 head green cabbage
2 carrots
1 onion
5 tablespoons mayonnaise

1 tablespoon Dijon mustard
3 tablespoons cider vinegar
2 teaspoons sugar
1 tablespoon salt

Shred cabbage and grate the carrots and onion. Combine mayonnaise, Dijon mustard, cider vinegar, sugar and salt and mix well. Pour over grated vegetables and toss well. Refrigerate before serving. Serves 6.

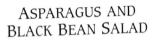

ASPARAGUS AND BLACK BEAN SALAD

A colorful and very tasty cold salad that is an excellent addition to any barbeque. The cilantro dressing gives it a wonderfully fresh flavor.

INGREDIENTS FOR SALAD:

1 pound fresh asparagus
1 16 oz can black beans, drained

2 tablespoons onion, chopped
1 tomato, chopped

INGREDIENTS FOR DRESSING:

3 tablespoons olive oil
2 tablespoons red wine vinegar
1 clove garlic, crushed

1 tablespoon cilantro, chopped
1/2 teaspoon ground cumin
Salt and pepper

Break off ends of asparagus and wash, removing scales if tough. Cut into 1 inch pieces. Place steamer basket in less than 1/2 inch water, making sure the water does not touch the asparagus. Cover and bring to a boil. Reduce heat and steam for 6 minutes. When asparagus has cooled, add black beans, tomato, and onion. Refrigerate for several hours. In a separate bowl, combine olive oil, red wine vinegar, garlic, cilantro, cumin and salt and pepper to taste. Shake well before pouring over asparagus and black beans. Serve on a bed of lettuce Serves 6.

A WORD ABOUT PARSLEY:

Parsley, most often used as a garnish, is very rich in vitamin C.

DESERT ORIENTAL SALAD

A touch of the Orient here in the Southwest. This makes a refreshingly light meal for a hot summer night.

INGREDIENTS FOR SALAD:

2 tablespoons sugar
1/2 cup sliced almonds
1/2 head iceberg lettuce
1/2 head romaine lettuce
1 cup chopped celery

2 green onions, chopped
1 11 oz can mandarin oranges, drained
1 avocado, sliced

INGREDIENTS FOR DRESSING:

2 tablespoons orange juice
1/4 teaspoon grated orange peel
1/4 teaspoon salt
1 tablespoon red wine vinegar

1 tablespoon sugar
1 tablespoon lemon juice
1/4 cup oil

Combine orange juice, grated peel, salt, oil, vinegar and sugar and mix well. In a small pan, heat sugar and almonds until sugar is dissolved and almonds are coated. Shred and mix lettuce, celery and onions, avocado and mandarin oranges. Pour dressing over all and top with almonds.

❖ ——————————— ❖ ——————————— ❖

SEDONA SQUASH SOUP

INGREDIENTS:

2 large onions, chopped
1/4 cup oil
4 1/2 cups vegetable broth
1/2 cup lentils
1 1/2 cups pureéd squash

1 teaspoon marjoram
1 teaspoon thyme
1/4 teaspoon pepper
Salt

Sauté onions in oil until tender. Add vegetable broth, lentils and squash, simmer for 30 minutes. Add marjoram, thyme, pepper and salt to taste. Simmer for 45 minutes. Serves 6.

❖ ——————————— ❖ ——————————— ❖

A WORD ABOUT CACTUS:

The pear shaped fruit of yellow spine prickly pear and the desert prickly pear cactus are the most flavorful of the cactus fruits. To use in sauces, dip fruit into boiling water for a moment then purée and strain.

Prickly Pear Salad

Picking the fruit from a prickly pear cactus is quite a challenge, but it is certainly worth the effort! Choose either yellow spine prickly or desert prickly pear cactus for the best fruit.

INGREDIENTS:

1/4 cup orange juice
1/3 cup 7-Up
1 teaspoon ginger root, grated
1 tablespoon lemon juice
2 tablespoons sugar

1 peach, peeled and sliced
1 pear, peeled and sliced
1 cup strawberries, sliced
1/4 cup prickly pear fruit, diced
Mixed salad greens

To prepare prickly pear, place fruit in boiling water for 1 minute, then dip in cold water. Use a knife to slice and peel skin, scraping off any needles. Combine orange juice, 7-Up, ginger root, lemon juice and sugar. Mix well and pour over fruit. Chill before serving on a bed of salad greens.

Sweet Potato Soup

INGREDIENTS:

4 large sweet potatoes, peeled
Chicken stock
2 green leeks, chopped
2 tablespoons butter

1 cup whipping cream
1/2 teaspoon white pepper
2 tablespoons chives, chopped
1 teaspoon thyme

Cut sweet potatoes into large pieces and place in a medium pot. Add chicken stock to cover. Melt butter and sauté leeks. Add to pot with sweet potatoes. Cook potatoes over medium heat until potatoes are done. Set aside to cool. Transfer potatoes to a blender or food processor and purée to a smooth consistency. Add cream to desired consistency. Add pepper and thyme to taste. Chill and garnish with chives before serving.

Citrus and Jicama Salad

INGREDIENTS FOR SALAD:

3 large oranges, cut in sections
2 pink grapefruit, cut in sections

1 large jicama, cut into cubes

INGREDIENTS FOR DRESSING:

1/4 cup dry red wine
1/4 cup oil

2 tablespoons orange juice
2 tablespoons honey

Combine oil, red wine, orange juice and honey in a jar. Cover and shake to mix. In a large bowl, mix oranges, grapefruit and jicama and toss with salad dressing. Serves 6.

❖——————————————❖——————————————❖

SALSA AND AVOCADO SALAD

Featuring avocados and bell peppers, foods of the Southwest, this salad combines the smooth and creamy texture of avocados with the crisp bite of tangy salad greens.

INGREDIENTS FOR SALAD:

1/4 pound romaine lettuce
1/4 pound radicchio
1/4 pound arugula
1 Belgian endive

4 ounces radish sprouts
2 avocados
4 ounces goat cheese, sliced

INGREDIENTS FOR SALSA:

1 red bell pepper, diced
1 orange bell pepper, diced
1 yellow bell pepper, diced
1 green onion, chopped
1 medium tomato, chopped

1 tablespoon cilantro, chopped
1 tablespoon olive oil
Juice from 1 lemon
Salt
Pepper

Peel and cut avocados in half, removing pit. In a small bowl, mix red, orange and yellow bell peppers, onion, tomato, cilantro, olive oil, lemon juice and salt and pepper to taste. Wash salad greens and arrange on 4 plates. Fill avocados half way with salsa. and cover with a slice of goat cheese. Broil for 2 minutes and place on lettuce to serve. Serves 4.

❖——————————————❖——————————————❖

PRICKLY PEAR VINAIGRETTE

INGREDIENTS:

4 prickly pear fruits, cleaned and puréed
6 ounces olive oil

2 ounces cider vinegar
2 tablespoons onion, chopped
1 teaspoon Dijon mustard

Combine purée with olive oil, cider vinegar, onion and Dijon mustard. Mix well and store covered. Makes 1 1/2 cups.

GREEN BEAN SALAD

My good friend, Lucia, serves this as a cool compliment to her spicy chorizo and rice recipe. This also goes well with grilled meats.

INGREDIENTS:

1 pound fresh green beans
1/3 cup olive oil
2 tablespoons lemon juice
Boiling salted water

2 cups water
1/2 medium red onion, sliced thin
1/2 teaspoon oregano
Salt and pepper

Wash green beans and snap off tips. Cut beans in diagonal slices. Cook beans in boiling salted water for 8 minutes, or until tender. Pour beans into a sieve and rinse well in cold water. Drain. Beat olive oil and lemon juice in a small bowl and pour over beans. Add salt and pepper to taste. Toss well. Bring 2 cups water to a boil in a small pan. Slide sliced onions into water and stir. Drain immediately. Place onion slices over beans.

❖————————————❖————————————❖

ORANGE AND ONION SALAD

INGREDIENTS:

2 red onions, cut into rings
1 large orange, cut in chunks
1 can tangerine slices, drained

1 cup sunflower seeds
1 head lettuce, shredded

Toss onions, orange, tangerine, sunflower seeds and lettuce. Top with fruit salsa or a light vinegarette. Serves 4.

❖————————————❖————————————❖

CHRISTMAS EVE SALAD

A lovely salad that is traditionally served in Mexican households on Christmas Eve. Serve on a beautiful tray for a festive presentation.

INGREDIENTS FOR SALAD:

3 oranges, peeled
3 limes, sliced thin
3 carrots, peeled, julienned,
blanched 1 minute and chilled
2 ripe bananas, sliced and
sprinkled with lime juice

1 jicama, peeled and julienned
5 large beets, cooked, julienned
and chilled
1 head romaine lettuce, shredded
1/2 fresh pineapple, sliced in 2
inch strips

INGREDIENTS FOR DRESSING:

1/4 cup white vinegar
3 tablespoons orange juice
1 tablespoon lime juice
1 teaspoon salt
1 teaspoon sugar

1 clove garlic
1/4 teaspoon paprika
1/8 teaspoon white pepper
2/3 cup vegetable oil
3/4 cup pine nuts

Blend garlic, vinegar, orange and lime juice, salt, sugar, paprika and pepper until smooth. Add oil in a steady stream and mix until creamy. Heat 2 tablespoons dressing in a medium skillet and sauté nuts until golden brown. Drain on paper towels to absorb excess oil. Combine oranges, limes, carrots, bananas and jicama in a large bowl. Pour the dressing, reserving 1/3, over top and toss gently. Add remaining dressing to beets and toss. Arrange fruits and vegetables decoratively over lettuce.

❖————————————————❖————————————————❖

Christmas Eve Salad

CHILI
A TEXAS TRADITION

Chili is commonly believed to have been the invention of a trail cook in Texas and dates back to the 1800's, although it is probable that long ago ancient Indians created meals consisting of meat and chiles. Chili lovers of today feel very strongly about the contents of their chili. The many Chili cooking competitions throughout the United States, and internationally, are testament to the fanaticism of chili lovers. Arguments abound over whether or not beans and other vegetables should be added to chili. Purists believe that only beef, chiles, onions and spices make up a "real" bowl of chili. Others, myself included, believe that the addition of other favorite foods can only make a good thing better. Following are a selection of recipes for you to choose from.

❖ ———————————————— ❖ ———————————————— ❖

DALLAS CHILI

This hearty chili is guaranteed to satisfy the appetite of even the biggest Texan. Serve with corn bread and a Lone Star Beer.

INGREDIENTS:

5 slices bacon, chopped	1 tablespoon chili powder
2 onions, chopped	1 teaspoon oregano
1 clove garlic, chopped	1 1/2 teaspoons cumin
1/2 pound ground pork	1 teaspoon salt
1 pound ground beef	2 6 ounce cans tomato paste
4 canned green chiles, chopped	3 cups water

Cook bacon in large chili pot. When bacon is thoroughly cooked remove and place on a paper towel to drain excess oil. Saute onions and garlic in bacon grease. Add beef and pork and cook, scrambled, until brown. Add chiles, chili powder, oregano, cumin, salt, tomato paste, and water. Mix well. Bring to a boil. Reduce heat and simmer for 1 1/2 hours, stirring often. Add bacon and simmer for 1/2 hour. Serves 4.

❖ ———————————————— ❖ ———————————————— ❖

MEXICAN CHILI WITH PORK

A more flavorful and filling meal is hard to find. This is an excellent way to use up left over pork roast.

INGREDIENTS:

3 1/2 pounds boneless pork, cut in bite sized cubes
4 medium tomatoes, quartered
2 7 oz cans green chiles, cut in strips

1 large onion, chopped
2 cloves garlic, minced
1 teaspoon oregano
1/4 teaspoon cumin
1 teaspoon salt

Place pork in a large pot and cover with water. Bring to a boil and let simmer over reduced heat for 40 minutes. Drain pork and place in a large skillet. Brown the meat and remove any fat. Add onions and garlic and cook until onions become tender. Add tomatoes, chiles, oregano, cumin and salt. Cover skillet and cook over medium heat for about 10 minutes. Uncover and continue cooking for 20 minutes. Serves 6.

RANCH CHILI

INGREDIENTS:

4 Anaheim chiles, roasted, seeded and chopped
3 jalapeño chiles, seeded and sliced
1 pound Italian sausage
1 large onion, chopped
1 clove garlic, minced
4 tomatoes, chopped

1 8 ounce can tomato sauce
1 cup frozen corn
1 teaspoon salt
1 teaspoon pepper
1 cup Cheddar cheese, shredded
1 cup Monterey Jack cheese, shredded

Slice or scramble sausage and brown over medium heat. Drain off excess oil. Add onion and garlic and sauté until the onion becomes tender. Add chiles, tomatoes, corn, sauce and salt and pepper. Simmer for 45 minutes over medium heat, stirring occasionally. Add 3/4 cup of each cheese and stir until melted. Use extra cheese to garnish.

CHILI STEW

INGREDIENTS:

1 quart cooked beans
2 tablespoons chili powder, dissolved in 5 ounces water

2 tablespoons oil
Salt
Pepper

Add oil to hot boiled beans. Salt to taste. Add dissolved chili powder. Simmer over medium-low heat for 45 minutes, stirring often.

CHICKEN CHILI

This wonderful chili, also called White Chili because of the use of chicken instead of beef, is a favorite with chicken lovers everywhere.

INGREDIENTS:

1 1/2 cups onion, chopped
1/2 cup green bell pepper, chopped
2 tablespoons oil
1 clove garlic, minced
2 tablespoons chili powder
2 tablespoons cumin
1 teaspoon oregano
4 cups cooked chicken meat, cut in bite sized pieces
1 cup water
1/2 teaspoon red pepper
1/4 teaspoon black pepper
1 tablespoon Worcestershire sauce
1 tablespoon Dijon mustard
1 14 ounce can stewed tomatoes
1 1/2 cups chicken broth
1 12 ounce bottle chili sauce
1 16 ounce can kidney beans
1 1/4 cups avocado, peeled and diced
1 1/4 cups red onion, chopped

Sauté onion and bell pepper in oil until tender. Add garlic, chili powder, oregano and cumin. Cook, stirring for 3 minutes. Add chicken, 1 cup water, red pepper, black pepper, Worcestershire sauce, mustard, tomatoes, chicken broth and chili sauce. Bring to a boil. Cover and simmer over medium heat for 20 minutes. Add beans, cook for 10 minutes. Garnish each bowl with diced avocado and red onion. Serves 8.

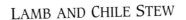

LAMB AND CHILE STEW

Here is another satisfying one-pot meal perfect for a cold desert night.

INGREDIENTS:

2 lbs lamb, cut in cubes
1 medium onion, sliced
2 tablespoons oil
1/8 teaspoon garlic powder
1 16 oz can plum tomatoes
1 celery stalk, chopped
1 1/2 cups corn, fresh or frozen
1 7 oz can green chiles
1 cup beer
1 teaspoon oregano
1/2 teaspoon cumin
Salt and pepper

Cook lamb in oil, browning on all sides. Remove lamb from pan and reserve oil. Add onion, garlic powder, celery and salt and pepper to taste in reserved oil. Cook until tender. Mix in tomatoes, corn, chiles, beer, oregano, cumin and lamb, stirring often. Bring to a boil. Cover and simmer on medium-low heat for 1 3/4 hours, until meat is tender. Serves 6.

EASY DOES IT CHILI

This is an easy-on-your-stomach chili for those of you who are hesitant to try the really hot and spicy types of chili.

INGREDIENTS:

1 medium onion, chopped
2 teaspoons butter
1 pound ground beef
1 tablespoon ground mild red chile
1 tablespoon ground hot red chile
1/2 teaspoon cumin

2 cloves garlic, minced
2 10.5 ounce cans tomato soup
1 10.5 ounce can onion soup
2 16 ounce cans kidney beans, drained
1 teaspoon oregano

Sauté onion in butter. Add ground beef, ground chile, oregano, cumin and garlic and mix well. Cook, scrambling meat, until brown. Add tomato soup, onion soup and beans. Bring to a boil. Simmer over medium heat for 1 hour, stirring often. Serves 4.

CHICKEN MEATBALL CHILI

The Italian plum tomatoes and celery give this different chili a flavor your mouth will never forget.

INGREDIENTS:

1 large celery stalk, chopped
1 medium onion, chopped
Oil
3/4 cup bread crumbs
1 egg
2 pounds ground chicken
2 tablespoons chili powder

3 carrots, sliced thin
1 28 ounce can Italian plum tomatoes, undrained
3 16 ounce cans kidney beans, drained
Salt and pepper
Water

Sauté onion and celery in oil, until tender. Add celery and onion mixture to bread crumbs and add ground chicken, egg, 1 1/2 teaspoons salt and 1/4 cup water. Shape chicken mixture into 1 1/2 inch balls. Cook meatballs in 2 tablespoons oil, until browned. Place browned meatballs in a separate bowl, reserving oil in skillet. In the skillet, cook carrots until tender. Add chili powder, tomatoes with liquid, 3/4 teaspoon salt, and 2 cups water. Bring to a boil. Return meatballs to skillet and simmer on low for 10 minutes. Stir in kidney beans and cook over medium heat for 20 minutes. Serves 8.

TERESA'S TERRIFIC CHILI

My very good friend, Teresa Martin, contributed this recipe. When she makes it sans beans, our close friend, Susan, loves it too!

INGREDIENTS:

1 1/2 pounds ground turkey
1 cup cooked pinto beans
1/2 cup green pepper
4 tablespoons green chile, diced

4 3/4 cups canned tomatoes, crushed and drained
2 tablespoons chili powder

Brown ground turkey. Add onions and pepper and cook until peppers are tender. Add beans, chile, tomatoes and chili powder and mix well. Simmer over low heat for 35 minutes. Serves 4.

TOMATILLO CHILI

The combination of poblano chiles and tomatillos gives this chili a wonderfully rich flavor.

INGREDIENTS:

1 1/4 pounds ripe tomatillos, peeled and seeded
6 poblano peppers
1 1/2 pounds pork, cubed
1 cup onion, chopped
1/2 teaspoon garlic powder
2 teaspoons cumin

2 teaspoons oregano
1/2 cup cilantro, chopped
1 tablespoon lemon juice
1/4 cup plain yogurt
Salt
Pepper

In a large pot cover tomatillos with water and bring to a boil. Cook for 8 minutes, until tender. Drain, reserving 1 cup fluid, and set aside. Brown pork in a skillet, stirring often to brown evenly. Remove meat from the skillet and, using remaining oils, sauté peppers and onion. Cook for 5 minutes before adding pork. Add tomatillos, reserved fluid, cumin, garlic, oregano and salt and pepper, stirring to mix. Bring mixture to a boil and simmer on low heat for 5 minutes. Top with a dollop of yogurt.

A WORD ABOUT CHILES:

Poblano chiles, dark green in color and slightly heart shaped, become Ancho chiles when ripened and dried and have a nice smoky flavor.

DOCTOR'S CHILI

My optometrist, Dr. Terri Giese, was kind enough to contribute this recipe. She can take care of your appetite as well as your eyes!

INGREDIENTS:

3 pounds ground beef or turkey
2 cloves garlic, minced
2 medium onions, chopped fine
1 green pepper, chopped fine
1 stalk celery, chopped fine
2 teaspoons oil
2 14 ounce cans stewed tomatoes, undrained
1 15 ounce can tomato sauce
1 6 ounce can tomato paste

2 15 ounce cans of kidney beans, drained
1/4 cup tomato/chili salsa (see recipe page 19)
1 ounce chili powder
1 4 ounce can diced green chiles, undrained
1/2 cup water
Salt and pepper

In a dutch oven, sauté garlic, onions, pepper and celery in oil until tender. Add meat, one pound at a time. Stir over medium heat until meat loses red color. Drain. Add water, stewed tomatoes, tomato sauce, tomato paste, kidney beans, chili salsa, chili powder, and green chiles, stirring often. Simmer for 2 1/2 to 3 hours, stirring often. Add salt and pepper to taste.

BEEF AND VEGETABLE CHILI

It's the extra vegetables and spices that give this chili its special flavor. Serve with chile corn bread and a glass of sangria.

INGREDIENTS:

3 pounds ground beef
1 cup onions, chopped
1 green pepper, chopped
2 stalks celery, chopped
2 carrots, chopped
1 cucumber, chopped
1 zucchini, chopped
1/8 teaspoon garlic powder
1 10 oz can of tomato sauce

1 16 ounce can of tomatoes, chopped
1 16 ounce can pinto beans
1/2 teaspoon parsley
1/4 teaspoon saffron
1/4 teaspoon rosemary
1 teaspoon salt
1/2 teaspoon pepper
1 tablespoon Tabasco sauce

In a large pan cook beef, onions, green peppers, celery, carrots, cucumber, zucchini, and garlic powder until vegetables become tender. Simmer over low heat for 1 hour. Add tomato sauce, chopped tomatoes, pinto beans, parsley, saffron, rosemary, salt and pepper and Tabasco sauce. Cook for 3 hours adding water for desired consistency. Serves 6.

VEGETARIAN CHILI

Here is another recipe given to me by my friend Cathy Orlowski. She is a vegetarian who's natural order of entertaining always involves food.

INGREDIENTS:

1 16 ounce can of pinto beans, drained
1 16 ounce can of kidney beans, drained
9 cloves garlic, unpeeled
8 large onions, chopped
10 fresh mushrooms, chopped fine
1 large zucchini, chopped fine

1 28 ounce can peeled tomatoes, with fluid
4 tablespoons butter
1 1/2 teaspoons chili powder
1 teaspoon cumin
1/2 teaspoon cayenne pepper
1/2 cup Monterey Jack cheese, shredded
Salt

Cover garlic cloves with water in a small saucepan and cook over high heat until the water boils. Drain and cool garlic for 5 minutes. Peel and chop. Sauté onions in butter in a large pan until tender and light brown. Add garlic and sauté for 5 minutes. Add zucchini and mushrooms and sauté until tender. Add tomatoes with fluid, chili powder, cumin, cayenne pepper and salt to taste. Bring mixture to a boil. Simmer over medium heat for 50 minutes. Add kidney and pinto beans, cook for 30 minutes. Garnish each serving with shredded Jack cheese. Serves 6.

TURKEY CHILI

This is an easy to make, basic chili recipe that uses turkey instead of beef. Of course, you can always substitute beef or chicken if desired.

INGREDIENTS:

1 pound coarsely ground turkey
3 tablespoons bacon drippings
1/2 cup onions, chopped
1 1/4 cups canned tomatoes
4 cups canned kidney beans

1 teaspoon seasoned salt
1 teaspoon sugar
2 tablespoons chili powder
1/4 cup Monterey Jack cheese, shredded

Sauté onion in bacon drippings in a medium pot, draining excess oil. Add ground turkey, cook until meat loses pink color. Add canned tomatoes, kidney beans, salt, sugar and chili powder. Cover and simmer on low for 1 hour. Garnish with cheese. Serves 8.

UNCLE LEONARD'S CHILI

This tasty contribution is from our good friend Sue Adams. Her Uncle Leonard was quite famous for his chili recipe and after my first bite, I found out why.

INGREDIENTS:

2 pounds ground beef
5 large onions, chopped
4 stalks celery, chopped
2 large cans whole tomatoes
1 can water
2 cans chili beans
4 tablespoons chili powder

1 1/2 tablespoons salt
1 1/2 teaspoons pepper
1/2 tablespoon garlic salt
1/2 tablespoon seasoning salt
1 tablespoon vinegar
1 tablespoon sugar

In a large pot, brown ground beef and onions, drain excess oil. Add celery, tomatoes, water, chili beans, chili powder, salt, pepper, garlic salt, vinegar, seasoning salt and sugar. Bring to a boil. Simmer on low heat for 1 1/2 hours. Serves 8.

❖─────────────❖─────────────❖

RED MESA CHILI

I use beef tenderloin instead of stew beef. Tenderloin is more expensive, but its tenderness and great taste can be worth the extra expense.

INGREDIENTS:

2 pounds beef stew meat
2 tablespoons oil
1 cup water
1 can green chiles, drained
Water
2 cloves garlic, minced

1 teaspoon salt
1 tablespoon oil
1 onion, chopped fine
1 tablespoon flour
1 teaspoon oregano
1/4 teaspoon cumin

Prepare meat by cutting into bite sized pieces and browning in 1 tablespoon oil. Add water and simmer for 1 hour, covered. Purée chiles in a blender with 1/2 cup broth from meat. Press purée through a sieve to remove bits of peel. Add purée to meat and broth. Mash garlic with salt to a paste. Cook garlic paste and onion in 1 tablespoon oil. Cook until onion is tender. Add flour and stir 1 minute. Add onion mixture, oregano and cumin to meat mixture. Simmer, covered, for 1 to 2 hours. Add salt and pepper to taste. Serves 6.

Grilled Tuna with Papaya Salsa and Black Bean Cakes

LUCIA'S LUSCIOUS CHILI

Lovely Lucia offers her favorite chili recipe along with all of her help on this book. Thanks lots Lish!

INGREDIENTS:

1 pound lean ground beef	1 15 ounce can tomato sauce
1/2 cup celery, chopped fine	1 tablespoon chili powder
1 small onion, chopped fine	Salt
2 cloves garlic, minced	Pepper

Cook ground beef, celery, onion and garlic until beef turns brown. Drain excess fat. Add tomato sauce, chili powder and salt and pepper to taste. Simmer over medium heat for 25 minutes or until desired thickness is achieved. Serves 4.

TEXAS CHILI

I've often thought Texans have the best chili recipes around and this recipe is a Texan favorite. And of course, there are no beans in this chili.

INGREDIENTS:

2 pounds beef, cut into bite size pieces	1 teaspoon oregano
1 1/2 cups onion, chopped	1/2 teaspoon red pepper
1 cup green bell pepper, chopped	1/3 cup masa harina or cornmeal
3 serrano chiles, seeded and chopped	1 16 ounce can stewed tomatoes, undrained
1 tablespoon oil	1 can beef broth
1/2 teaspoon garlic powder	1 can beer
2 tablespoons chili powder	1/3 teaspoon salt
1 teaspoon cumin	1/2 teaspoon hot sauce
	2 tablespoons lemon juice

In a heated skillet, cook meat until brown, stirring often to prevent sticking. Drain and set aside. Sauté onion, bell pepper and serrano chiles in oil until tender. Add meat, chili powder, cumin, oregano, garlic and red pepper. Sprinkle masa harina over meat mixture. Mix well. Add tomatoes, beer, salt, hot sauce and beef broth and bring to a boil. Simmer over medium heat for 1 1/2 hours. Add lemon juice and simmer for 30 minutes or until meat is tender. Serves 6.

CHACO CHILI

It's the wonderful selection of spices added to this chili that makes it so special. Add your own mix of spices for a unique variation.

INGREDIENTS:

5 medium onions, chopped
1/4 teaspoon seasoning salt
1/4 teaspoon pepper
4 pounds ground beef
5 cloves garlic, minced
1 tablespoon oregano
2 teaspoons woodruff
1 teaspoon cayenne pepper
2 tablespoons paprika

3 tablespoons cumin powder
3 teaspoons oregano
2 teaspoons chili powder
1 teaspoon Tabasco sauce
3 10 ounce cans tomato sauce
1 teaspoon tomato paste
3 tablespoons flour
Vegetable oil

Sauté onions in oil. Add salt and pepper. Place onions in a large chili pot. Brown beef, using oil if necessary. Add garlic and 1 tablespoon of oregano. Add cooked meat to the onions in the chili pot. Mix together woodruff, cayenne pepper, paprika, cumin, chili powder, and remaining oregano. Add spice mixture to chili pot. Add Tabasco sauce, tomato sauce and tomato paste to chili pot. Add enough water to cover meat. Simmer on low heat for 2 hours. Bring chili to a boil. To thicken, make a paste by mixing a little water and flour. Stir in paste, stirring constantly until desired thickness is achieved. Serves 8.

❖―――――――――――――❖―――――――――――――❖

WESTERN WYOMING CHILI

INGREDIENTS:

1 pound dry pinto beans
3 pounds ground beef
1 large green pepper, chopped
1 large onion, chopped
2 cloves garlic, crushed

6 large tomatoes, chopped
1 tablespoon cumin seed
1/4 teaspoon Tabasco sauce
4 tablespoons chili powder
2 cups water

Clean pinto beans by rinsing thoroughly. Place beans in a shallow pot and cover with water. Soak overnight. Brown meat, add green pepper, onion and garlic. Add tomatoes and cook, covered, for 30 minutes. Add pinto beans, cumin seed, Tabasco, chili powder and water. Stir to mix. Simmer on low for 2 hours. Serves 6.

MAIN DISHES
FLAVORS OF THE SOUTHWEST

With the heavy Mexican influence in Southwest cooking and the influx of people from all over the world, it's no wonder that our choice of foods is varied. In this chapter you will find many traditional Southwestern dishes, some with new and updated flavors, along with recipes created by newcomers who have brought family recipes and their own regional specialties which have become the new favorites of the Southwest. My personal favorites are the *Chicken Chile Cheeseburger* (page 66), the very savory *Taos Pork* (page 57) and *Chile Fettuccine* (page 60) which simply melts in your mouth. Enjoy!

❖————————————————❖————————————————❖

BARE CHILE RELLENOS

There are many ways to stuff a chile, this is just the first of many great recipes found in this chapter.

INGREDIENTS FOR MARINADE:

1 7 ounce can whole green chiles 1/8 teaspoon garlic powder
1/3 cup olive oil Salt
3 tablespoons wine vinegar Pepper

INGREDIENTS FOR FILLING:

7 ounces cooked chicken 1 tablespoon parsley
1 medium potato, cubed 1 tablespoon cilantro
1 medium carrot, cubed 1/3 cup mayonnaise
1/4 medium onion, diced 3 tablespoons sour cream

In a shallow pan combine olive oil, wine vinegar, garlic powder, salt and pepper to taste. Peel and seed chiles, leaving stem and chile whole. Cut a slit down the side of each chile and place in the marinade for 2 1/2 hours. Cook the diced carrot and potato in enough water to cover for 8 to 10 minutes or until tender. Cut cooked chicken into bite sized squares and add potatoes, carrots, parsley, onion, cilantro, sour cream, mayonnaise and 3 tablespoons marinade. Salt and pepper to taste. Remove chiles from marinade and place on paper towels to drain excess marinade. Fill each chile with chicken mixture. Garnish with sour cream or parsley and serve. Serves 6.

Chicken Enchiladas

CHICKEN ENCHILADAS

A Southwest favorite and a traditional Mexican dish, this chicken enchilada recipe is always a smashing success.

INGREDIENTS:

3 cups cooked chicken, shredded
7 ounces green chili salsa, fresh or canned
1 4 ounce can chopped green chiles
2 1/2 cups heavy cream
1/2 cup Jack or Colby cheese
12 corn tortillas
1/2 teaspoon salt
1/2 head lettuce, shredded
12 olives

In a large bowl, combine cooked chicken, chiles and salsa. In a shallow pan, mix cream and salt. Soften corn tortillas by dipping into a pan of heated oil, then place on paper towels to absorb extra oil. Dip each softened tortilla into the cream mixture and fill with the chicken. Roll filled tortillas and place in an ungreased baking dish. Pour extra cream over enchiladas. Top with grated cheese and bake, uncovered, for 25 minutes. Garnish with shredded lettuce and olives. Serves 6.

❖————————————————❖————————————————❖

VERDE VALLEY MEAT LOAF

This is an excellent meal to make ahead and freeze. Serve with Corn Bread and Five Bean salad for a complete meal.

INGREDIENTS:

1 1/2 pounds ground beef
1 cup soft bread crumbs
1 cup canned, undrained tomatoes
3 tablespoons dried onion flakes
1 7 ounce can green chiles, drained, seeded and chopped
1 1/4 teaspoons salt
1/4 teaspoon garlic salt

Preheat oven to 375° F. Combine ground beef, bread crumbs, tomatoes, onion flakes, salt, chiles, and garlic salt. Mix thoroughly. Place mixture in a large loaf pan and press lightly. Bake for 1 hour. Serves 6.

❖————————————————❖————————————————❖

ZUCCHINI AND CHILE CASSEROLE

This savory casserole can be served as a side dish or as a meal all by itself when served with warm tortillas or French bread.

INGREDIENTS:

4 cups zucchini, sliced
1 onion, chopped
1 clove garlic, minced
1/2 cup canned green chiles, drained and chopped
1/2 cup canned cream corn
2 tablespoons butter

2 tablespoons hot water
1 cup Cheddar cheese, shredded
4 eggs, beaten
1 tablespoon fresh parsley, chopped
Salt
Pepper

Preheat oven to 350°F. Grease a 1 to 2 quart casserole dish. In a medium skillet, sauté onion in butter until tender. Add zucchini, garlic, chiles and water. Reduce heat and cook for about 7 minutes, or until zucchini is tender, stirring often to prevent sticking. Add corn, 1/2 cup cheese, eggs, parsley and salt and pepper to taste. Place zucchini and chile mixture in casserole dish and top with remaining cheese. Bake for 45 minutes or until set. Serves 6.

TAOS PORK

This zesty pork dish must be tasted to be believed. Serve with a side of beans or a fresh salad for a hearty meal.

INGREDIENTS:

2 pounds pork, trimmed and cubed
1 tablespoon chili powder
2 10 oz cans enchilada sauce
2 cups water
2 tablespoons flour

1/2 teaspoon cumin
2 cloves garlic, minced
1 teaspoon sugar
1 teaspoon salt
1 teaspoon pepper

In a large skillet, cook pork until lightly browned. Add chili powder and flour. Stir to mix well. Add enchilada sauce, water, cumin, garlic, sugar, salt and pepper and bring to a boil. Simmer, covered, for 1 1/2 to 2 hours. Add water to thin, if desired. Serves 6.

A WORD ABOUT CHILES:

There are a wide variety of chiles grown throughout the Southwest and Mexico. Chile flavors run from mild and sweet to hot, very hot and even hotter. The general rule is the larger the chile the more mild the flavor. Beware, however, as this is not always so. Every chile, even those picked from the same bush, has its own flavor and degree of heat. If you have a chile that's too hot, soak the chile in salt water for about 2 hours, make sure to rinse before using.

Following Pages: Baked Pork Loin

CHILE FETTUCCINE

This pasta dish is unlike any other you may have tasted. The smooth flavor of the fettuccine and the spicy taste of the sauce come together to make this an unforgettable experience

INGREDIENTS:

1 pound package fettuccine
1 clove garlic, minced
3/4 cup olive oil
3/4 cup fresh green chiles, roasted, peeled and sliced thin

1/2 cup red bell pepper, sliced thin
1/2 cup piñon nuts
1 cup Parmesan cheese, grated
Salt
Pepper

Cook fettuccine according to directions. In a large skillet, sauté garlic, chiles, red pepper and piñon nuts in olive oil. Mix with pasta and top with Parmesan cheese and salt and pepper. Serves 6.

LAMB WITH CHILE SAUCE

An excellent lamb dish, the chile sauce can be used on beef and chicken as well. Grill on the barbeque to get a smoky flavor.

INGREDIENTS:

5 pound leg of lamb, boned and flattened
1/3 cup olive oil
1 teaspoon salt
1 teaspoon pepper
2 medium onions, diced
2 cups chili sauce
1/2 cup lemon juice

1 teaspoon hot pepper sauce
2 tablespoons vinegar
1 tablespoon canned green chiles, minced
1 tablespoon brown sugar
1 teaspoon cumin
1 bay leaf, crushed

Rub lamb with olive oil and salt and pepper. In a medium sauce pan, combine onions, chili sauce, lemon juice, olive oil, hot pepper sauce, vinegar, chiles, sugar, cumin and crushed bay leaf and mix well. Cook over medium heat for 20 minutes. Place flattened lamb on a grill, over medium-low coals. Cook, turning every 15 minutes, for 2 hours. Baste lamb with chile mixture every 10 to 15 minutes. Serves 6.

A WORD ABOUT AVOCADOS:

When avocados yield to gentle pressure they are ripe and can be stored in a cool refrigerator for 4 or 5 days.

CHILE BURGERS

Burgers are certainly one of the most barbequed foods in the Southwest. Serve on whole wheat buns with grilled corn on the cob.

INGREDIENTS:

1 pound lean ground beef
2 7 oz cans of whole green chiles, seeded, deveined and chopped
Salt

Whole wheat hamburger buns
Pepper
Salsa

Combine ground beef and chopped chiles and form into burgers. Salt and pepper burgers before grilling to desired doneness. Place burger on the bottom bun and spoon a small amount of salsa on top of burger before topping with bun. Serves 6.

STUFFED PEPPERS

This is a very simple and light meal that can be attractively presented by slicing the pepper in half lengthwise, without disturbing the stem.

INGREDIENTS:

4 red or green peppers, cored and seeded

2 cups chicken stock

INGREDIENTS FOR STUFFING:

2 onions, sliced
2 tablespoons butter
1/4 pound mushrooms, chopped
2 cups cooked rice

2 tablespoons parsley, chopped
1 teaspoon oregano
Salt
Pepper

Preheat oven to 350°F. To prepare stuffing, sauté onion in butter until tender. Add mushrooms, cooked rice, parsley, oregano and salt and pepper to taste. Cook for 5 minutes. Place peppers in a deep baking dish and fill with stuffing. Pour stock over top and bake for 45 minutes to an hour, until tender. Serves 4.

A WORD ABOUT TEQUILA:

Tequila is made from the maguey, a succulent plant that is quite large and has long, thick leaves. Premium tequila is aged in oak casks and has a beautiful golden color.

CHILI SKILLET

Using frozen vegetables makes this very quick to prepare. If you have extra time use fresh mixed vegetables instead.

INGREDIENTS:

1 pound ground beef	1/4 teaspoon salt
1 16 oz can tomatoes, loosely cut and undrained	1 16 oz package frozen seasoned mixed vegetables
1 tablespoon flour	1 cup Cheddar cheese, shredded
1/2 teaspoon chili powder	

In a large skillet, cook beef until brown, drain. Combine tomatoes, flour, chili powder and salt and mix well. Mix frozen vegetables and tomato mixture into meat. Bring to a boil. Cover and simmer on low heat for 8 minutes, stirring often. Spread cheese over top and cover until melted. Serve with warm tortillas and Spanish rice. Serves 5.

❖————————————❖————————————❖

PAELLA

Nothing can compare to this wonderful seafood Paella! Serve with warm sourdough bread for a satisfying meal.

INGREDIENTS:

1 cup rice	1/3 cup carrots, chopped
1/4 cup olive oil	15 mussels, in shells
2 patties chorizo	10 clams, in shells
1 cup clam juice	10 raw shrimp, in shells (fresh or frozen)
1 cup chicken broth	Saffron
1 cup peas	

Pour oil and rice into a large skillet or Dutch Oven and cook until rice becomes a golden brown. Add chorizo, chicken broth, peas, carrots, clam juice and a dash of saffron to rice. Mix well. Drop mussels, clams and shrimp on top of rice and bring mixture to a boil. Simmer, covered, for 20 minutes. Transfer to a large bowl before serving. Serves 8.

❖————————————❖————————————❖

A WORD ABOUT SAFFRON:

Saffron, a native of the Mediterranean, is most often used in Spanish, South American, and French dishes. Saffron is the most expensive spice in the world and is used more for color than for flavor. Saffron pieces can be used in cooking but it is most often used ground.

DUMPLING STEW

This zesty stew has the added advantage of corn dumplings to give it a down-home flavor your family will love.

INGREDIENTS FOR STEW:

1 pound lean ground beef
2 medium onions, chopped
2 potatoes, peeled and diced
2 cups pinto beans, cooked
2 large tomatoes, chopped

1 tablespoon butter
2 teaspoons chili powder
2 teaspoons salt
Water

INGREDIENTS FOR DUMPLINGS:

3/4 cup whole kernel corn, fresh or canned
1 cup flour
1 teaspoon baking powder

3 tablespoons cornmeal
White Pepper
Salt

In a large pot, combine at least 3 cups water with diced potatoes, cooked pinto beans and salt. In a medium skillet, heat butter and sauté onion until tender. Add ground beef and cook until brown. Drain excess oil. Add tomatoes and chili powder and simmer over low heat for 5 minutes. With a large serving spoon, spoon meat mixture into pot with potatoes. Bring to a boil and simmer over low for 25 minutes. Using a blender, grate corn well. In a medium mixing bowl, combine flour, baking powder, cornmeal and corn. Add water, if necessary, to keep dough from crumbling, but keeping dough stiff. Add dumpling mixture by the spoonful to chili and simmer, covered, for 5 to 10 minutes. Serves 6.

❖————————————❖————————————❖

BAKED PORK LOIN

INGREDIENTS:

1 pork loin roast, about 3 pounds
1 tablespoon chili powder
2 cloves garlic

1/2 teaspoon oregano
1 16 ounce bottle of Cola drink
Salt and pepper

Preheat oven to 350°F. Mix chili powder, garlic, oregano and 1/4 of the cola drink in a blender. Salt and pepper the roast before placing in a skillet to brown on all sides. Place roast in a baking pan and spread with cola and spice mixture. Add remaining cola and bake for 2 hours, or until meat thermometer reaches 170°F. Baste often with pan mixture. Serve with pan fluid as a sauce. Serves 6.

ROAST TURKEY

It's the jalapeño cornbread stuffing that gives this traditional bird it's Southwestern flavor. A definite taste treat for turkey lovers everywhere.

INGREDIENTS:

1 18 to 20 pound turkey, thawed	Salt
Seasoned salt	Pepper

INGREDIENTS:

3 stalks celery, diced	1/4 cup butter
1 onion, diced	2 loaves cornbread, dried and
5 jalapeño peppers, cleaned and	crumbled
seeded, diced	3 cups chicken stock

Remove giblets and neck and reserve for other uses. Preheat oven to 325°F. Rinse and season turkey with seasoning salt, salt and pepper. Sauté celery and onion in butter until tender. In a medium mixing bowl, combine sautéed celery and onion with the jalapeño peppers, cornbread crumbs and 2 cups of chicken stock, adding more stock if necessary. Stuff turkey tightly and place in a large roasting pan. Cook for approximately 5 hours, basting regularly. Turkey is done when leg moves up and down freely and juice runs clear. Serves 12.

❖ ——————————————— ❖ ——————————————— ❖

MARINATED SIRLOIN STEAK

INGREDIENTS:

1 cup olive oil	1 teaspoon soy sauce
2 pounds sirloin steak, trimmed	1/4 teaspoon Tabasco sauce
2 tablespoons dry mustard	1 tablespoon fresh lime juice
2 tablespoons Worcestershire	Salt
sauce	Pepper
2 cloves garlic, minced	

Combine olive oil, reserving 2 tablespoons, dry mustard, Worcestershire sauce, garlic, soy sauce, Tabasco sauce, lime juice and salt and pepper to taste. Pour mixture over meat, which has been placed in a glass container, and refrigerate overnight. Turn meat often. Preheat oven to 375°F. Two hours before roasting, remove meat from refrigerator and bring to room temperature. Using reserved oil, sear meat on both sides in a very hot skillet and then place in oven to cook until a meat thermometer reads 135°F. Slice and serve with pan drippings as sauce. Serves 6.

SABANA DE RES

Pound this beef tenderloin until very thin, like a bed sheet, which is what "sabana" means in Spanish.

INGREDIENTS:

2 pounds beef tenderloin
1 cup olive oil
1/2 onion, minced
1 teaspoon paprika
1/2 teaspoon cayenne pepper

1/2 cup minced green olives
2 cloves garlic, minced
1 teaspoon oregano, chopped
1 teaspoon basil, chopped
1/2 teaspoon cracked pepper

INGREDIENTS FOR SAUCE:

1/2 cup onion, julienned
1/2 poblano chile, julienned
2 cloves garlic, minced
1 tablespoon olive oil
2 cups heavy cream

1/2 cup Oaxaca cheese, shredded
4 tablespoons cilantro, chopped
Salt
Pepper

Combine olive oil, onion, paprika, cayenne, olives, garlic, oregano, basil and cracked pepper. Mix well and set aside. Cut beef tenderloin into four steaks. Place steaks between sheets of wax paper and pound each steak with a meat mallet until steaks are only 1/8 inch thick. Brush flattened meat, on one side only, with marinade and let sit for a couple of hours. Sauté onion, poblano chile and garlic in olive oil until tender. Add cream and reduce until thickened. Remove pan from stove and add cheese, cilantro and salt and pepper to taste. Cook meat, or *sabana*, in a large, very hot skillet. Cook for about a minute on each side. Roll steaks and cover with sauce before serving. Serves 4.

❖————————————❖————————————❖

TOMATO AND PEPPER CHOPS

INGREDIENTS:

6 pork or lamb chops
1 tablespoon olive oil
7 medium tomatoes, chopped

3 green peppers, chopped
2 tablespoons flour
Salt and pepper

Sift flour and add salt and pepper to taste. Coat chops with flour mixture and heat oil in a skillet. Brown chops and add tomatoes and peppers and cover. Simmer for 25 minutes. Serves 6.

SHREDDED BEEF BURRITOS

Burritos can be made with almost anything and can be a great way to use leftover meat, poultry or fish.

INGREDIENTS:

1 pound beef stew meat
1 1/2 cups water
Salt and pepper to taste
1/2 onion, chopped
1 clove garlic, minced
2 tablespoons oil
3 medium tomatoes, peeled and chopped

1 green pepper, chopped
1 tablespoon chili powder
4 large flour tortillas
1 1/2 cups refried beans
Salsa
1 1/2 cups Monterey or Cheddar cheese, shredded
Shredded lettuce

Combine beef, water and salt and pepper to taste in a large pot. Bring to a boil and simmer, covered, on low heat for about 2 hours, or until beef is tender. Set aside to cool. Once meat is cool enough, drain and reserve broth. Shred meat with a fork. In a medium skillet, sauté onion and garlic in oil until tender. Add tomatoes and simmer for 10 minutes. Add green pepper, chili powder and shredded meat. Add 1/2 cup broth and salt and pepper again to taste. Simmer on low for 15 minutes, until green pepper is tender. Heat refried beans and spread a couple of tablespoons of beans on flour tortilla, add shredded beef, cheese, lettuce and salsa. Fold bottom of tortilla up, about 3 inches, then fold left or right side over and roll to finish. Serve on shredded lettuce and top with cheese. Serve with red or green sauce if desired. Serves 4.

❖ ———————————————————— ❖ ———————————————————— ❖

CHICKEN CHILE CHEESE BURGERS

INGREDIENTS:

1 pound ground chicken
2 7 ounce cans chiles, chopped
Salt and pepper

1/2 pound Monterey Jack cheese slices
Hamburger Buns

Combine ground chicken, chopped chiles and salt and pepper to taste. Form 4 good sized patties and grill for about 20 minutes, or until done. Just before serving, place a layer of chiles over burgers then top with a slice of Jack cheese. Allow cheese to melt before serving. Serves 4.

Fajitas, an original Southwestern entree.

FAJITAS

INGREDIENTS:

3 pounds sirloin steak, trimmed
1/2 cup lime juice
3 tablespoons oil
3 cloves garlic, minced
1 1/2 teaspoons ground cumin
1 teaspoon oregano
4 small onions, sliced

3 bell peppers, sliced
15 flour tortillas
Salt and pepper
Sour Cream
Guacamole
Refried Beans
Salsa

Cut steak into 3 inch by 1 inch strips and place in a glass bowl. Add lime juice, oil, garlic, cumin, oregano, and salt and pepper to taste. Mix well, making sure to coat all beef. Add onion and bell pepper slices and cover. Refrigerate overnight or for at least 4 hours. Drain meat and vegetables. Heat oil in large skillet and sauté meat and vegetables until cooked to your liking. Serve with sour cream, guacamole, beans and salsa. Serves 6.

FATTENED CHILES

These stuffed chiles, or Chile Rellenos, should be stuffed so full that they could be called fat! The raisins and almonds give this a unique flavor.

INGREDIENTS:

2 medium onions, chopped
2 tablespoons oil
1/8 teaspoon garlic powder
1/2 pound ground beef
1/2 pound ground pork
2 medium tomatoes, chopped
1 teaspoon salt

1/2 teaspoon pepper
4 tablespoons sliced almonds
4 tablespoons raisins
8 canned whole chiles, seeded
4 eggs
1/2 cup flour
Oil for frying

Sauté onions in oil until tender. Add garlic powder and ground meats and cook until scrambled and brown. Add tomatoes, salt, pepper, almonds and raisins. Cook on low. In a separate pan, beat egg whites until stiff and add beaten egg yolks. Stuff chiles with meat filling. Roll stuffed chiles in flour and dip in egg batter. Fry the chiles in oil at 375°F, until lightly browned. Place on paper towels to absorb excess oil before serving. Serve with refried beans or rice. Serves 8.

❖ ——————————— ❖ ——————————— ❖

MEXICAN CHILE PIE

INGREDIENTS:

6 corn tortillas
1 cup vegetable oil
1 onion, chopped
3 tomatoes, chopped
1 cup chicken, diced

3 poblano chiles, skinned, seeded
and sliced in strips
1 cup cream or half and half
1/2 cup Cheddar cheese, shredded
1/2 teaspoon salt

Heat oil in a small pan and fry each tortilla until firm but not crisp. Place on paper towels to absorb excess oil. In a larger pan, heat 2 tablespoons oil and cook onions and tomatoes for 20 minutes. Add salt and set aside. Preheat oven to 400°F. Grease a pie plate and make a bottom layer using 3 tortillas. Pour half of the tomato mixture over the tortillas then layer with diced chicken. Make another layer with the poblano chiles and top that with 1/2 cup cream. Place half of the cheese over cream and top with remaining tortillas. Finish by layering remaining tomato mixture, cream and cheese. Bake at 400°F for 15 to 20 minutes. Let cool for 10 minutes before serving in pie shaped pieces. Serves 4 to 6.

BEEF STEW

This slow-cooking beef stew is so good it simply melts in your mouth! Reheated, it also makes great leftovers.

INGREDIENTS:

2 pounds beef stew meat	1 bay leaf
1 cup water	1/4 teaspoon whole allspice
4 tomatoes	5 peppercorns
1 onion	1/4 teaspoon sugar
1 clove garlic, minced	Salt
1 tablespoon oil	

Cut meat into bite size pieces. Place meat in a large saucepan and add water and salt to taste. When water begins to boil, reduce and simmer, covered, for 1 hour. Quarter tomatoes and onion and place in a blender with garlic. Blend until smooth. Heat oil in a medium pot and add tomato blend, bay leaf, allspice, peppercorns and sugar. Bring to a boil then simmer for about 15 minutes. Add beef to tomato mixture and simmer for 1 to 2 hours. Serve over rice or by itself. Serves 6.

HIGH DESERT POT ROAST

This is unlike any pot roast you've ever had before. The brown sugar, wine vinegar and chiles really make it flavorful.

INGREDIENTS:

3 pounds beef chuck steak	2 teaspoons salt
1 1/4 cups dry white wine	2 cloves garlic, minced
4 tablespoons wine vinegar	3 tablespoons butter
5 green chiles, cleaned and chopped	1 onion, chopped
4 tablespoons brown sugar	3/4 cup beef broth
	3 tablespoons tomato paste

Combine white wine, wine vinegar, chiles, brown sugar, salt and garlic, mix well. Place beef in a shallow pan and pour marinade over top. Cover and refrigerate overnight, turning several times. When you are ready to cook, drain beef and reserve marinade. In a large skillet, brown beef in butter on both sides. Add 1 to 2 cups of marinade, onion, broth and tomato paste. Cover and simmer for 1 1/2 hours, until the beef is very tender. Simmer, uncovered, for 1/2 hour to allow sauce to thicken. Serve pot roast sliced, with sauce served separately. Serves 8.

Seafood Kabobs

SEAFOOD
FROM CEVICHE TO SALMON

Seafood has always been a big part of Mexican cooking which means it also plays an important role in the kitchens of the Southwest. The ready availability of fresh fish throughout most of the Southwest means you can make a fish taco almost as easily as a beef taco, or you can prepare the spicy *Snappy Red Snapper* (page 76) or the smooth essence of *Cold Lobster with Apricot Sauce* (page 75) with a visit to your local market. Grilling fish on the barbeque almost year round is a definite advantage of Southwest living. Try a topping of flavorful salsa over your favorite fish, adding an exciting touch of Southwest flavor!

❖————————————————❖————————————————❖

CEVICHE

Ceviche can be made with almost any kind of fish, or a combination of fish and shellfish, and is often served for lunch or as an appetizer.

INGREDIENTS:

1 1/2 pounds white fish fillets   1 cup fresh lime juice

INGREDIENTS FOR MARINADE:

1 1/2 onions, chopped   1 4 ounce can jalapeño peppers,
4 serrano chiles, chopped   chopped
3 tomatoes, chopped   1/4 cup Worcestershire sauce
3/4 cup parsley, chopped fine   1 tablespoon oregano
3 cups ketchup   2 tablespoons cilantro, chopped
1 1/2 cups olive oil   Salt

Cut fish into 1 by 1 inch square pieces. Place fish in a non-metal bowl and add all but 2 tablespoons of the lime juice. Let sit for 1/2 hour. Drain and rinse and return fish to bowl. To prepare marinade, combine onion, serrano chile, tomato, parsley, remaining lime juice and cilantro. Add the ketchup, oil, jalapeño chiles, Worcestershire sauce, oregano and salt. Pour over fish and cover. Refrigerate overnight and drain most of the marinade before serving with tortilla chips or crackers.

❖————————————————❖————————————————❖

A WORD ABOUT FISH:

Fish cooks very rapidly so be sure not to over cook. Constant supervision of grilled fish is necessary. Fish is cooked completely when translucent flesh turns opaque and flaky.

WHITE FISH IN BLACK SAUCE

The seasonings, along with the raisins, beer and wine, come together to create this mouth watering delight.

INGREDIENTS:

1 1/2 pounds white fish fillets
2 tablespoons butter
2 carrots, diced
2 stalks of celery, diced
1 medium onion, chopped fine
1 bay leaf
1/2 teaspoon dried thyme
2 sprigs parsley
1/2 teaspoon salt
1/2 teaspoon pepper

1 1/2 cups dark beer
1 cup red wine
3 tablespoons lemon juice
2 teaspoons sugar
1/4 cup chopped walnuts
1/4 cup seedless raisins
2 tablespoons plum jam
1/4 cup blanched almonds, chopped

Sauté carrots, celery and onion in butter until tender, about 5 minutes. Add bay leaf, thyme, parsley, salt and pepper. Add 1 cup beer, wine, lemon juice, sugar, walnuts, raisins and jam. Stir to mix and cook for 15 minutes. If the sauce becomes too thick, add more beer. Place fish in a skillet and spoon sauce over top. Poach over medium heat for about 15 minutes, until fish is done. Place fish fillets on individual plates and spoon sauce over top, discarding bay leaf. Garnish with almonds.

❖ ——————————————— ❖ ——————————————— ❖

TRIPE WITH CHILE

This sumptuous meal takes a little time to prepare but tastes wonderful.

INGREDIENTS:

1 pound tripe
2 tablespoons bacon drippings
3 potatoes, peeled and sliced very thin
1 onion, diced

1 clove garlic, minced
1/2 teaspoon salt
1 7 ounce can green chiles, drained and chopped
2 tomatoes, sliced

Rinse tripe before placing in a pan, covering with water and simmering for several hours. When tripe has been cooked for at least 3 hours, drain and cut into 1/2 inch strips. Preheat oven to 325°F. Heat bacon drippings in a medium skillet and add sliced potatoes, onions, garlic, salt, chiles and tripe, cooking until browned. Add tomatoes. Cover and bake for 35 minutes at 325°F. Serves 4.

LOBSTER WITH APRICOT SAUCE

This lobster dish, served cold, is my version of a similar recipe I tasted in London several years ago.

INGREDIENTS:

4 1 to 2 pound lobsters	Sprig of mint
4 apricots, halved	

INGREDIENTS FOR SAUCE:

1/2 cup onion, diced	1 tablespoon lemon juice
1 tablespoon oil	1 1/2 cups mayonnaise
1 1/2 teaspoons curry powder	2 1/2 tablespoons apricot preserves
3/4 cup red wine	
1 bay leaf	2 tablespoons heavy cream
1 teaspoon tomato paste	Dash of Tabasco sauce

To prepare lobster; using a large pot, place a rack inside pot to sit 2 to 3 inches above the bottom. Add water to just below rack. Cover and bring water to a boil. When steam begins to escape from pot, add lobsters. Cover and begin timing. When steam begins to escape from lid, cook 12 to 14 minutes. Remove lobsters and chill for 30 minutes. Remove meat from lobster tail and claws and set aside. To prepare sauce; sauté onion in oil in a medium pan until onion becomes light brown. Add curry powder and cook for 1 minute. Add wine, bay leaf, tomato paste, lemon juice and Tabasco. On high heat, reduce mixture until 3/4 cup remains. Remove bay leaf and discard. Pour mixture into smaller bowl and chill for 5 minutes. Combine mayonnaise, wine and onion mixture and apricot preserves and purée in a food processor or blender until smooth. Add salt to taste. Slice meat from lobster tails down center, opening wide. Spoon sauce over middle of lobster tail and around meat. Arrange meat from claws on side, on top of sauce and serve. Garnish with apricot halves and mint.

❖──────────────❖──────────────❖

A WORD ABOUT SHELLFISH:

Live oysters, mussels, clams and scallops should have tightly closed shells. Shells should not be cracked, chipped or broken in any way. If any shells are open, tap the shell to discover if fish are alive. Live shellfish will close up tight if disturbed. Do not cook dead, unshucked clams, mussels, oysters or scallops. Shucked clams, mussels and oysters should be plump and surrounded by clear, opalescent liquid. All fresh shellfish should always have a mild odor.

SALMON IN SHALLOT SAUCE

The combinations of flavors and textures give this savory salmon dish an elegant appeal. Serve with your favorite white wine.

INGREDIENTS FOR SALMON:

5 pounds salmon	2 bay leaves
2 cups white wine	2 small onions
1 cup water	8 peppercorns

INGREDIENTS FOR SHALLOT SAUCE:

1/2 cup dry white wine	1/2 teaspoon salt
1 teaspoon shallots, diced	1/2 teaspoon white pepper
2 cups heavy cream	1 cup capers

To prepare shallot sauce; place wine and shallots in a saucepan and bring to a boil over medium heat. Cook until mixture has reduced to 1/2, about 5 minutes. Add cream and salt and white pepper and cook over low heat, stirring often with a wire whisk. Cook until mixture reduces to 1 1/2 cups and strain through a sieve. Set aside. To prepare salmon add wine, water bay leaves, onions and peppercorns to the bottom of a fish poacher and bring to a boil. Wrap salmon in cheesecloth or place on a rack in poacher before placing in the water. Lower heat and cook for 10 to 15 minutes. When inserted knife comes out clean, fish is done. Place salmon on individual serving plates and spoon shallot sauce over most of the fish and onto the plate. Garnish lavishly with capers. Serves 6.

❖———————————————❖———————————————❖

SNAPPY RED SNAPPER

INGREDIENTS:

1 pound red snapper fillets, cut into 1/4 inch strips	1/2 cup bell pepper, sliced
	2 fresh jalapeño peppers, sliced
1/2 cup onion, sliced	1 clove garlic, minced
1/2 cup celery, sliced	3 tablespoons olive oil

Heat olive oil in a large skillet and add onion, celery, bell pepper, jalapeño pepper and garlic. Sauté for 4 minutes before adding strips of fish. Turn fish strips until cooked on all sides and serve, spooning vegetables over the top. Serves 4.

PASTA WITH MUSSELS

This delightful pasta dish, with its creamy sauce, is a wonderful meal to serve when entertaining friends.

INGREDIENTS:

10 pounds mussels	3 cups heavy cream
2 1/2 cups dry white wine	1/2 cup parsley, chopped fine
5 shallots, diced	1/4 cup dry sherry
1 bay leaf	1 pound linguine
1 1/2 teaspoons pepper	1 teaspoon salt

Rinse mussels thoroughly, discarding any that are already open and making sure to remove the beards. Add wine, shallots, bay leaf and pepper in a large pot. Bring to a boil and add mussels. Cover pot and steam on high heat until they open, about 2 minutes. Remove pot from heat and set aside. When mussels cool, pour liquid into a bowl. Remove mussel shells. Strain mussel fluid through several layers of cheesecloth into pan. Bring fluid to a boil and reduce it down to 1/2 cup. Skim if necessary. Add cream, stirring constantly, and let it boil down to half the volume. Add 1/4 cup parsley and salt. Add sherry and shelled mussels. Cover and cook over extremely low heat. Prepare pasta as directed on package. Drain and transfer to large serving bowl. Add sauce and mix gently. Garnish with remaining parsley. Serves 6.

❖───────────────❖───────────────❖

SHRIMP AND SCALLOP CEVICHE

INGREDIENTS:

1/2 pound shrimp, shelled, deveined and diced	1/4 cup fresh cilantro, chopped
1/2 pound scallops, diced	1/4 teaspoon crushed dry red pepper
1 cucumber, peeled and diced	Lemon juice
1 carrot, diced	Salt
1 scallion, diced	Pepper

Place diced scallops and shrimp in a bowl and rinse well. Add lemon juice to cover and refrigerate for 2 1/2 to 3 1/2 hours. In a medium mixing bowl combine cucumber, carrot, scallion, cilantro and red pepper. When shrimp and scallops have become opaque, remove from lemon juice and add to the bowl of vegetables. Add the juice of one fresh lemon and salt and pepper to taste. Serves 6.

AHI TUNA WITH PAPAYA SALSA

What a taste treat this is! There is nothing like this colorful combination for a dinner party or special celebration.

INGREDIENTS:

6 7 ounce Ahi steaks

INGREDIENTS FOR SALSA:

2 papayas, peeled, seeded and chopped
1 small red onion, diced
1 serrano chile, seeded and diced
1 small red bell pepper, seeded and diced

1 tablespoon water
2 tablespoons peanut oil
1/2 cup fresh mint leaves
1/2 cup lime juice
Salt
Pepper

To prepare salsa; in a medium pan, combine onion, chile, bell pepper, water and oil. Simmer over low heat for 10 minutes. Remove to medium mixing bowl. Blanch mint leaves by dipping in boiling water for one minute. Cool in ice water and dry with paper towels. Dice mint leaves and add to vegetable mixture. Add papayas, lime juice, salt and pepper to taste. Set aside to marinate for 1 hour. To prepare steaks; grill steaks on a hot grill for 2 to 3 minutes per side. Top with salsa and serve.

❖————————————————❖————————————————❖

SWORDFISH KABOBS

INGREDIENTS:

1 pound swordfish fillets
1/4 cup lime juice
1/4 cup vegetable oil
1 tablespoon cilantro, chopped
1/2 teaspoon salt

1 clove garlic, minced
1/2 jalapeño, seeded and chopped
1 cup pineapple chunks
2 zucchini, cut into 1/2 inch slices
1 red bell pepper, cut in squares

Cut fish into 3/4 inch chunks. Combine lime juice, oil, cilantro, salt, garlic and jalapeño pepper in glass bowl. Mix well and add fish chunks. Cover and refrigerate for at least 2 hours, turn often. Remove fish and reserve marinade. Alternately thread fish, pineapple, zucchini and bell pepper on 11 inch skewers, leaving a little room between each piece. Place full skewers over a heated grill, or on a rack in a broiler pan. Brush with marinade, turning and brushing often for about 5 minutes, or until fish becomes flaky. Serve with rice or a side of beans. Serves 4.

WHITE FISH IN TOMATILLO SAUCE

This flavorful dish can be quickly prepared. if tomatillos are not available use small green tomatoes.

INGREDIENTS:

1 1/2 pounds white fish fillets
3 tablespoons lime juice

3 tablespoons oil
1/2 teaspoon salt

INGREDIENTS FOR SAUCE:

1 pound tomatillos
3 green onions, chopped
1 clove garlic
1 tablespoon parsley

1 mild green pepper, cleaned
and seeded
2 teaspoons oil
Salt

Remove husks from tomatillos and wash well. In a medium saucepan, pour 1/2 inch water and add fresh tomatillos. Bring to a boil then cover, reduce heat, and cook until tomatillos become tender, about 10 minutes. Drain and cool. Place tomatillos, green onions, garlic, parsley and chile in a food processor or blender and purée. In a medium saucepan, heat 2 teaspoons oil and add purée. Salt to taste and bring to boil. Simmer over reduced heat, uncovered, for 15 minutes. Prepare fish by sprinkling with lime juice and salt. Let stand for 45 minutes. In a large skillet, heat 3 tablespoons oil and cook fish for 1 minute on each side. Add sauce and cover. Simmer for 5 minutes or until fish becomes flaky. Serves 6.

❖————————————————❖————————————————❖

WHITE FISH TACOS

INGREDIENTS:

1 pound white fish fillets
1 medium tomato, diced
1/4 cup green onion, diced
2 tablespoons canned green chiles
2 tablespoons lemon juice

1 cup hot cooked spinach,
chopped
8 taco shells
1 cup sour cream
Salt and pepper

Poach fish with lemon juice and water to cover until fish becomes opaque and flakes easily with a fork. Combine tomato, green onion, chile and salt to taste. Drain fish and cut into small chunks, removing any bones or skin. Place equal amounts of fish on each taco shell, add hot spinach and top with tomato mixture. Garnish with sour cream and serve with beans or rice. Serves 8.

POULTRY
FROM ROASTED TO BLACKENED

Poultry, the perfect meat for almost everybody, is gaining popularity in kitchens around the world. Here in the Southwest it is used more than any other meat and has long been a favorite to generations of cooks, from the earliest Native Americans and Mexicans to newcomers from around the globe. A healthful alternative to beef, chicken is often cooked skinless and served without heavy sauces or gravies. Recipes offered here are easily prepared, good for you, and taste wonderful.

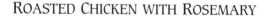

ROASTED CHICKEN WITH ROSEMARY

Serve this elegant and savory dish with Caramel Glazed Carrots and save the leftovers for Chicken Enchiladas.

INGREDIENTS:

3 2-to-2 1/2 pound broiling chickens
4 to 5 sprigs fresh rosemary
1/4 cup butter
1/2 cup white wine
1 cup chicken stock

1 cup heavy cream
1 teaspoon arrowroot mixed with 1 tablespoon water to form paste
Salt
Pepper
Trussing needle and string

Preheat oven to 375°F. Place a sprig of rosemary inside each chicken and truss them. In a large baking or casserole dish, melt butter and brown chickens on all sides. Place on one side and add wine, half the stock and remaining rosemary leaves, stripped from stems. Add salt and pepper and cover pan. Bake for 30 to 40 minutes or until the chickens are tender. Test by pricking thigh, if no pink juice escapes, chickens are done. Turn from side to side during cooking. Remove trussing strings and place on a platter. Keep warm. Add stock to cooking juices and bring to a boil. Work juices and rosemary leaves through a sieve to purée. Return sauce to pan and add cream. Bring just to a boil and add arrowroot paste until sauce thickens slightly. Taste to season before spooning sauce around chickens, or serve on the side. Serves 6.

A WORD ABOUT CENTERPIECES:

Centerpieces can add fun, flair and beauty to any table setting. A simple straw cowboy hat, resting upside down, can be just the thing to fill with fresh flowers for a lovely Southwestern centerpiece.

Grilled Chicken and Coleslaw

BLACKENED CHICKEN SALAD

The spices add a touch of Cajun to this delightfully spicy chicken dish. Serve with a glass of cool ice tea.

INGREDIENTS:

1 pound boneless chicken breasts
1 bunch spinach
1 head romaine lettuce
1 cucumber, sliced
1 medium red onion, thinly sliced
1/2 cup sunflower seeds
1 teaspoon garlic powder

1/2 teaspoon onion powder
1/2 teaspoon oregano
1/2 teaspoon ground red pepper
1/2 teaspoon black pepper
1/2 teaspoon salt
2 cups croutons (see recipe 31)
Salad dressing

Remove the skin from chicken. Combine garlic powder, onion powder, oregano, red pepper, black pepper and salt, rub all over chicken. Place seasoned chicken on a broiler pan and place under broiler for about 8 minutes, until chicken is cooked thoroughly. Let chicken cool and cut into bite sized pieces. Tear spinach and romaine lettuce into bite sized pieces. In a large bowl, combine spinach, lettuce, onion rings, cucumber, croutons and sunflower seeds with chicken pieces. Pour your favorite dressing over the top and serve. Serves 4.

❖———————————————❖———————————————❖

CHICKEN IN CHIPOTLE CHILE SAUCE

INGREDIENTS:

1/2 cup green chiles, diced
1 4 pound chicken, cut in pieces
1 16 ounce can stewed tomatoes
5 canned chipotle chiles
1 small onion, sliced thin
1/2 teaspoon garlic powder
1 teaspoon oregano
1 1/2 teaspoons cumin

1/2 teaspoon cloves
1/4 teaspoon pepper
1 tablespoon chicken bouillon granules
3 cups water
2 bay leaves
1 teaspoon salt

Combine green chiles, undrained tomatoes, chipotle chiles, garlic, cumin, oregano, clove and pepper. Place mixture in a blender and purée. Add bouillon granules. Set aside. In a large pot, place chicken, water, bay leaves and salt. Bring to a boil. Cover and simmer on low heat for 45 minutes. Drain broth. Add chipotle chile sauce and onion to chicken. Stir and coat chicken with sauce. Bring to a boil. Simmer on low heat for 20 minutes. Serve with a salad and corn on the cob. Serves 4.

TURKEY AND MUSHROOM LOAF

Besides being a great way to use up left over turkey, this is a great tasting dish that should be served with a colorful selection of vegetables.

INGREDIENTS:

1 2 pound loaf of crusty bread	1 egg, beaten
3 tablespoons melted butter	

INGREDIENTS FOR FILLING:

2 cups cooked turkey, shredded	1/2 teaspoon thyme
1/2 pound mushrooms, sliced	1/2 teaspoon tarragon
1 stalk celery, diced	1/4 teaspoon nutmeg
6 tablespoons butter	1 tablespoon parsley, chopped
1 onion, diced	Salt
1 1/2 tablespoons flour	Pepper

To prepare bread; preheat oven to 350°F. Cut off the top of the loaf of bread and remove soft bread inside. Melt 2 tablespoons butter and brush inside of the loaf with butter. Brush with beaten egg. Bake for 8 minutes, until bread is crispy and light brown. To prepare filling; sauté onion and celery in 2 tablespoons butter until tender. Stir in flour and remove pan from heat. Add chicken stock, return to stove and bring to a boil, stirring often. Simmer for 2 to 3 minutes. Remove from heat and add turkey, thyme, tarragon and nutmeg and parsley. Sauté mushrooms in remaining butter until tender. Spread a layer of mushrooms in the bottom of the loaf before adding turkey mixture. Top with remaining mushrooms and replace lid. Bake for 5 to 10 minutes, until loaf becomes very hot.

LIME CHICKEN

INGREDIENTS:

6 chicken breasts	2 teaspoons white wine vinegar
3 limes	Salt
2 teaspoons basil, chopped	Pepper
4 tablespoons olive oil	

Remove skin from chicken. Salt and pepper chicken and place in a baking dish. Using a citrus zester, pare thin strips of rind from limes. Combine lime juice, rind and wine vinegar with 4 tablespoons of olive oil. Pour mixture over chicken and marinate for several hours. Preheat oven to 375°F. Baste chicken with lime mixture and bake for 30 minutes.

BREAKFAST
FROM HUEVOS TO TRAILCAKES

B reakfast is easily my favorite meal of the day. When you try any of the wonderful breakfast recipes to follow you will see what is so very special about breakfast in the Southwest. Don't miss my version of *Huevos Rancheros* on this page or my fruity *Sunny Breakfast Juice* (page 86). Nutritionists say breakfast is the most important meal of the day, and I heartily agree!

SUNSHINE SCRAMBLE

This very flavorful egg dish should be served with warm flour tortillas, refried beans and a tall glass of orange juice.

INGREDIENTS:

15 large eggs	1 small onion, diced
3 tablespoons oil	1/4 cup cilantro, chopped fine
1/2 cup jalapeño peppers, diced	Salt
1/2 cup red bell pepper, diced	Pepper

Beat eggs and add jalapeño peppers, red bell pepper, onion, cilantro and salt and pepper to taste. In a large skillet, heat oil and add egg mixture. Stir often, scrambling eggs and cooking evenly. Serves 6 to 8.

HUEVOS RANCHEROS

A traditional Mexican breakfast, this ranch style egg dish makes an exciting meal. Serve with refried beans and warm flour tortillas.

INGREDIENTS:

4 eggs	2 green chiles, peeled, mashed and
1 tablespoon onion, minced	strained
2 tablespoons oil	1/2 teaspoon oregano
1/8 teaspoon garlic powder	1 teaspoon salt
1 8 ounce can tomato sauce	1 teaspoon pepper

In a large skillet, sauté onion in oil until tender. Add garlic, oregano, green chile, tomato sauce and salt and pepper. Simmer for 5 minutes, letting flavors blend. Poach or fry eggs and cover with sauce.

Chocolate Chip and Orange Muffins

SUNNY BREAKFAST JUICE

You will start your day with more enthusiasm when you begin with this high energy breakfast drink.

INGREDIENTS:

1 banana, peeled
1 egg (optional)
1 cup orange juice

1 tablespoon wheat germ
1/4 cup nonfat powdered milk
4 or 5 strawberries

Put banana, egg, orange juice, wheat germ, powdered milk and strawberries into a blender and whirl until smooth. Pour into large glass and enjoy! Makes 2 cups.

❖ ——————————————— ❖ ——————————————— ❖

EGGS AND SALSA

Fresh salsa really adds a punch to this egg dish. Serve for brunch with refried beans and corn bread.

INGREDIENTS:

6 eggs
6 corn tortillas (see page 94)

3 tablespoons butter

INGREDIENTS FOR SALSA:

3 large tomatoes
1 4 ounce can green chiles
1 medium onion

1/4 cup fresh cilantro
3 tablespoons lime juice

To prepare salsa; place tomatoes, drained chiles, onion, cilantro and lime juice in a blender. Blend for 30 seconds, leaving some texture to salsa. To prepare eggs; place heated corn tortillas on serving plate, overlapping two per plate. Fry eggs in butter, two or three at a time. Just before dishing up, add a small amount of salsa to frying eggs. Spoon eggs and salsa over waiting corn tortillas. Serves 3.

❖ ——————————————— ❖ ——————————————— ❖

A WORD ABOUT OREGANO:

Mexican oregano grows native over most of New Mexico. With lavender blossoms and large, flat leaves, this musky oregano is an authentic flavor of Mexican cooking. If it is unavailable, it should be left out, not replaced by the Greek or Italian type of Oregano.

FRUIT BOWL

Fruit is natures candy, and a favored snack. Try this with any selection of fruits, adding wheat germ or granola cereal.

INGREDIENTS:

1 ripe papaya, pitted and sliced
1 pint strawberries, stemmed and sliced
1 orange, peeled and sliced
1 red apple, cored and sliced

1 bunch seedless grapes, picked from stem
1 1/2 cups low fat plain yogurt
1/4 cup shredded coconut

Mix yogurt with papaya, strawberries, orange slices, grapes and apple slices. Garnish with shredded coconut and serve in small bowls. Add your favorite granola if you desire. Serves 4.

❖────────────────❖────────────────❖

TRAILCAKES

INGREDIENTS:

1 cup pancake mix
1 tablespoon oil
1 cup milk
1 egg

1/3 cup Quaker 100% Natural Cereal
1/2 teaspoon sugar

Preheat pan or griddle. Combine pancake mix, oil, milk, egg and sugar. Stir until smooth and add cereal. Pour mixture, in desired amounts, on preheated pan or griddle. When cakes bubble on top, and bottoms are golden brown, turn pancake and cook other side. Serve with syrup or preserves. Serves 4.

❖────────────────❖────────────────❖

COTTAGE CHEESE PANCAKES

INGREDIENTS:

1 cup cottage cheese
1/2 cup whole wheat flour
2 teaspoons oil

1/2 teaspoon vanilla
4 eggs

The night before, combine cottage cheese, whole wheat flour, oil, vanilla and eggs in a blender and blend until mixed. Refrigerate overnight. When ready to cook, pour onto heated grill. When tops bubble and bottoms are brown, flip and cook until light brown on both sides.

SIDE DISHES
FROM ANASAZI BEANS TO ARTICHOKES

Beans and rice are staples of the Mexican diet and are very important in the Southwestern diet as well. Vegetables, such as squash, corn, zucchini, potatoes, carrots and, of course, the ever present chile, are also very important ingredients in Southwestern cooking. Traditional dishes like *Refried Beans* (page 93) and *Sedona Rice* (page 92) are joined in this section with *Greens with Chiles* (page 92) and my *Western Potato Wedgies* (page 91) to help round out your next meal.

❖ ——————————————— ❖ ——————————————— ❖

CREAMED CORN WITH CHILES

This creamy corn and chile recipe makes a lively side dish for any meal. The combined flavors of poblano chiles and cheese adds an unusual dimension of flavor to the corn.

INGREDIENTS:

7 cups corn, fresh from the cob or frozen
4 poblano chiles, sliced
3/4 cup Swiss cheese, cubed

1 onion, chopped
1 clove garlic, minced
4 tablespoons butter
Salt and pepper

Heat butter and sauté chopped onion and garlic until tender. Add corn, poblano chile, Swiss cheese and salt and pepper to taste. Cook over low heat, stirring often, for 30 minutes. Serves 4.

❖ ——————————————— ❖ ——————————————— ❖

CHILI BEANS

INGREDIENTS:

1/2 pound pinto beans
4 1/2 cups water
1 teaspoon salt

1 teaspoon chili powder
1 medium onion, chopped
1/4 teaspoon crushed red pepper

Rinse beans, removing any foreign objects. Add water, bring to a boil. Cover and cook for 3 minutes. Cover and set aside to soak for 1 hour. Add salt, chili powder, red pepper and onion. Bring to a boil. Cover and simmer for 1 to 2 hours on low heat until beans are tender, stirring often.

Anasazi Beans

STUFFED ARTICHOKES

The impressive presentation of this excellent dish means it can easily be served as a main entree, especially for your vegetarian friends.

INGREDIENTS:

4 artichokes
1/4 cup white wine
1 1/2 cups vegetable stock

1 tablespoon butter
1/2 tablespoon flour

INGREDIENTS FOR FILLING:

3/4 pound mushrooms
3 tablespoons butter
1 medium onion, diced
1 medium carrot, diced
1/2 cup chopped ham

2 tablespoons parsley, chopped
1 teaspoon oregano
1 teaspoon marjoram
1/2 cup fresh breadcrumbs
Salt and pepper

To prepare artichokes; trim stalks of artichokes and, using scissors, trim leaves and tops to remove spines. Wash artichokes thoroughly and place in salted water. Bring to a boil. Boil for 35 to 45 minutes, until a leaf can be pulled away with little effort. Drain, rinse and cool. To prepare filling; chop mushrooms, reserving 4 large mushrooms. Sauté onion and carrot, in 1 tablespoon butter, until soft. Add chopped mushrooms and cook for 4 or 5 minutes, until all moisture has evaporated. Remove pan from heat and add ham, parsley, oregano, marjoram and enough breadcrumbs to make a firm mixture. Add salt and pepper to taste. Remove center leaves from artichokes and scoop out hairy chokes. To finish; preheat oven to 350° F. Fill center with mushroom mixture, topping with whole mushroom and pat of butter. Tie a string around artichokes to hold leaves in place and arrange artichokes in a deep baking dish. Pour wine and stock around artichokes and cover baking dish with lid or foil. Bake for 35 to 40 minutes, until tender. Place artichokes on a serving platter and keep warm. Mix butter and flour together and set aside. Strain cooking fluid before reheating. Whisk butter and flour mixture into cooking liquid to thicken. Simmer for 2 minutes and add salt and pepper to taste. Pour sauce around baked artichokes and serve. Serves 4.

GRILLED ACORN SQUASH

Using the barbeque is an easy and efficient way to prepare food. Cook this on the grill along with chicken, ribs or a nice big steak.

INGREDIENTS:

3 medium acorn squash	2 tablespoons water
3 tablespoons butter	Salt
1/4 cup brown sugar	Pepper

Rinse squash before cutting in half lengthwise. Remove seeds and, using a fork, prick flesh. Salt and pepper squash and place 1 tablespoon butter, 1 tablespoon brown sugar and 1 tablespoon water into each hollow of squash. Wrap in aluminum foil and place cut side up on grill. Cook over medium coals for 60 minutes, until tender. Remove foil and use a fork to raise squash. Sprinkle with remaining brown sugar and serve.

❖———————————❖———————————❖

WESTERN POTATO WEDGIES

I first tasted this dish while visiting friends in Knoxville, Tennessee, and soon adapted it to my own taste. I have prepared it for friends and family so much over the years they've become "Dorothy's Potatoes."

INGREDIENTS:

6 medium potatoes	1 small onion, chopped
1/4 cup butter	Salt
1/4 cup oregano, chopped	Pepper
1/4 cup parsley, chopped	

Preheat oven to 375° F. Scrub potatoes and slice into wedges. Melt butter. Put potato wedges and chopped onion in a baking dish and pour butter over the top, coating evenly. Sprinkle oregano, parsley, salt and pepper to taste over potatoes and bake for 45 minutes or until desired crispness is reached. Use a slotted spoon to turn potatoes occasionally. Serves 5.

❖———————————❖———————————❖

CARAMEL GLAZED CARROTS

INGREDIENTS:

10 carrots, peeled and cut in strips	1 tablespoon Madeira
1 cup beef broth	Water
1 1/4 cups packed brown sugar	Salt

Place carrots in a medium saucepan and add water to cover. Add a dash of salt to water and bring to a boil for 20 to 25 minutes. Set aside. Mix beef broth, brown sugar and wine in a medium saucepan and stir until sugar dissolves and mixture coats the spoon. Add carrots and cook for 5 minutes. Serve carrots and spoon caramel mixture over top. Serves 4.

SEDONA RICE

This rice dish has all the beautiful colors of Sedona. Serve with chicken, beef or seafood, either grilled or baked.

INGREDIENTS:

2 tablespoons butter	1 16 ounce can tomatoes
1 clove garlic, minced	1 13 ounce can chicken broth
1 large onion, chopped	Salt
1 1/4 cups uncooked rice	Pepper

In a medium sauce pan, sauté onion and garlic in butter until tender. Add rice, tomatoes, chicken broth, salt and pepper to taste. Bring to a boil and cover. Simmer for 15 minutes, until all the liquid is absorbed and the rice is tender. Serves 6.

GREENS WITH CHILES

The chiles give the greens an interesting flavor. This is proof that chiles really can be served with almost everything.

INGREDIENTS:

1 1/2 pounds fresh greens, swiss chard, mustard, or spinach	1/2 medium onion, chopped
1 7 ounce can green chiles, drained	1 clove garlic, minced
2 tablespoons butter	Salt
	Pepper

Wash greens well. Cook greens, in a small amount of boiling salted water, until tender. Drain and chop. Return to saucepan. Melt butter in a small skillet. Add chiles, onion and garlic and cook until onions are tender, about 5 minutes. Stir chile mixture into chopped greens. Heat thoroughly. Salt and pepper to taste. Serves 6.

REFRIED BEANS

Beans are the most commonly eaten food in the Mexican diet, and are equally popular throughout the Southwest.

INGREDIENTS:

1 pound red beans
1 1/2 quarts water

1 cup lard or bacon drippings
Salt

Soak beans overnight. Add more water to cover and add salt. Cook on very low heat until beans become tender. Using a potato masher, mash beans before adding 1/2 cup very hot bacon drippings or lard. Continue cooking until the fat has been absorbed, stirring often to avoid sticking. Heat additional fat in a frying pan and add beans. Cook and stir until beans become dry. Serves 6.

BLACK BEANS

INGREDIENTS:

2 cups dried black beans
1 onion, cut in half with one half chopped

2 cloves garlic, minced
1/4 cup lard
2 teaspoons salt

Place beans in a large saucepan and cover with hot water. Boil for 2 minutes then remove and let stand for 1 hour. Drain and rinse. Add more hot water to cover beans and bring to a boil. Reduce heat and add onion half and 3 tablespoons lard. Simmer, covered for 2 hours. Add salt. Cover and simmer for 2 more hours or until beans are tender. Add more hot water if needed to keep beans covered. Sauté chopped onion in remaining lard, until tender. Remove and discard onion half from beans. Add beans, including cooking fluid, to skillet with sautéed onion. Mash some, but not all, of the beans. Cook until thickened but not dry. Serves 8.

ANASAZI BEANS

INGREDIENTS:

2 cups Anasazi beans
4 cups water
1/4 cup oil
1 onion, chopped
1 clove garlic, minced

1/2 green bell pepper, chopped
1/2 red bell pepper, chopped
1 teaspoon chili powder
1 teaspoon salt

Sort and rinse beans. Place beans in water and cover. Soak overnight. Bring water to a boil. Simmer for 1 hour. Drain and reserve 1 cup liquid. Sauté onion and garlic in oil for 5 minutes. Add bean fluid, bell peppers, chili powder and salt. Cook on low heat for 45 minutes, stirring often. Add beans and simmer for 15 minutes. Serve hot or cold. Serves 6.

TORTILLAS AND BREAD
FROM BLUE CORN TO POLENTA

Tortillas are a versatile food with many uses in the Southwestern kitchen. An important ingredient in dishes such as Enchiladas, Tacos and Fajitas, tortillas are made from both corn and flour. Corn tortillas are the most common tortilla made in Mexico, while flour tortillas are more popular in Northern Mexico and the Southwestern United States. Once made, Tortillas can be fried for crisp shells, steamed to create Soft Tacos or baked for an endless array of dishes. In the Mexican kitchen tortillas never go to waste. Stale tortillas are used in casserole dishes or fried to make chips for salsas and dips. Blue corn tortillas have become popular again due to the many Santa Fe, New Mexico kitchens serving dishes featuring this traditional grain.

❖———————————————❖———————————————❖

CORN TORTILLAS

Masa harina can be bought at most grocery stores, or you can make your own by boiling lime-treated corn until soft and then grinding until it becomes a flour known as masa. It really is much easier to buy it!

INGREDIENTS:

2 1/2 cups masa   1 teaspoon salt
1 1/4 cups hot water

Combine masa and salt in a medium mixing bowl. Make a well in the middle and pour about 1/2 cup of water into well. Using your hands, mix well, adding water slowly, until a firm ball forms. Dough should feel springy to the touch with no cracks showing if pressed flat. If the dough is too wet and sticks to your hands, add more masa. Tear dough into small balls, about the size of an egg, one at a time and press between two sheets of wax paper. Using a rolling pin or tortilla press, flatten to about 6 inches in size. Cook tortillas, one at a time, on a skillet or comal until brown spots appear, about 1 minute per side. Makes 12.

❖———————————————❖———————————————❖

TO REHEAT TORTILLAS:

To soften a single tortilla, place tortilla on an ungreased warm griddle or skillet. Turn often until soft, about 30 seconds. To reheat a package of tortillas in a microwave oven, poke holes in the package and microwave for 1 minute. To fry tortillas, heat 1/2 inch oil in a skillet. When oil is hot, fry one tortilla at a time until tortilla becomes soft. Fold in half and hold slightly open with tongs to make U shaped. Fry until crisp.

FLOUR TORTILLAS

Flour tortillas were first introduced to Mexico by the Spaniards, who brought wheat to the New World. They are most popular in Northern Mexico and the Southwestern United States.

INGREDIENTS:

2 cups flour
1/4 cup lard

3/4 cup warm water
1/2 teaspoon salt

Combine flour and salt in a large mixing bowl. Add lard, using fingers, until well mixed. Add water, a little at a time, until dough forms a shiny ball. Pinch off balls of dough and roll out onto a floured board or pastry cloth to desired size. Cook on preheated griddle or comal for 1 to 2 minutes, until bubbles appear on top. Turn tortillas over and cook the other side. Serve warm. Makes 12 tortillas.

CHOCOLATE CHIP AND ORANGE MUFFINS

Muffins are an excellent choice for a light breakfast and these Chocolate Chip and Orange Muffins are especially tasty.

INGREDIENTS:

1/2 cup oil
1 egg, beaten
3/4 cup milk
1 teaspoon vanilla
2 cups flour
1 cup sugar

1 teaspoon salt
1 tablespoon baking powder
2 tbs orange peel, freshly grated
1 cup mini semisweet chocolate chips

Mix oil, beaten egg, milk and vanilla in medium mixing bowl. Combine flour, sugar, salt and baking powder. Add to egg and milk mixture and gently mix. Preheat oven to 400° F. Grease a muffin tray. Fold orange peel and chocolate chips into batter before pouring batter into the muffin cups. Bake for 20 minutes. Makes 12 muffins.

A WORD ABOUT TORTILLA UTENSILS:

A **comal** is a griddle used for baking or heating tortillas. **Bolillos** are short rolling pins that are two inches in diameter and used to roll flour tortillas to the correct thickness. They are also used to roll corn tortillas, however, a **tortilla press** works best when making corn tortillas.

POLENTA CAKES

These corn cakes are an excellent accompaniment to beef and chicken, as well as most egg or pasta dishes

INGREDIENTS:

1 quart water
1 teaspoon salt
1 cup yellow cornmeal, coarsely ground
1 teaspoon paprika
1/4 teaspoon cayenne pepper
2 tablespoons Parmesan cheese, grated
1/4 cup butter

Boil water with salt and gradually stir in corn meal. Cook over low heat, stirring often, for 15 minutes or until mixture pulls away from the sides of pan. Beat in paprika, cayenne pepper and grated Parmesan cheese. Spread mixture in a greased pan to form a layer 1/2 inch thick. Chill until set. Cut into squares and sauté in butter until brown on both sides.

❖―――――――――❖―――――――――❖

BLUE CORNBREAD WITH CHILES

Corn bread is the perfect accompaniment to any bowl of chili. Prepare extra for those really big appetites.

INGREDIENTS:

1 1/2 cups blue cornmeal
1/2 cup flour
1/2 teaspoon salt
1 tablespoon baking powder
1/4 cup onion, chopped
1 cup milk
1/2 cup butter, melted
3 jalapeño peppers, chopped
1 1/2 cups Monterey Jack cheese, shredded

Preheat oven to 350° F. Combine flour, cornmeal, baking powder, onion and salt. Add milk and butter and mix thoroughly. In a separate bowl combine cheese and jalapeños. Grease a medium sized baking pan and pour 1/2 of the batter into pan. Spread cheese and jalapeño mix evenly over batter. Pour remaining batter over cheese and cook for 1 hour.

❖―――――――――❖―――――――――❖

A WORD ABOUT CORN:

The history of the Southwest reflects the ancient Indians belief that man was created from corn by the gods. Today, corn is still considered an important crop and is the main ingredient in many recipes, from basic meals to desserts and beverages.

SOPAIPILLAS

A favorite at local carnivals and fairs, Sopaipillas are lightly fried and served warm with honey.

INGREDIENTS:

2 cups flour	3/4 cup warm water
2 teaspoons baking powder	Oil
1/2 teaspoon salt	Honey
1 tablespoon shortening	

Mix flour, baking powder and salt in a medium bowl. Add shortening, cutting in with a pastry blender or 2 knives, until evenly blended. Stir in warm water until ingredients become moist. Place dough on a lightly floured surface and knead dough until smooth, about 5 minutes. Wrap in plastic wrap and let rest for about 30 minutes. Cut dough in half and form each section into a ball. Roll out each ball of dough, on a floured surface, until round and about 1/8 inch thick. Cut in pie-shaped wedges. In a medium skillet, heat about 1 1/2 inches of oil to 400° F. Gently lay wedges of dough in hot oil. Cook until dough puffs up and becomes a light brown, turning once. Place cooked sopaipillas on paper towels to drain excess oil. Serve warm with honey. Makes 24 sopaipillas.

❖————————————❖————————————❖

ZUCCHINI BREAD

I can't think of any other type of bread that tastes so good, freezes well and makes as good a gift during the holidays as Zucchini Bread.

INGREDIENTS:

3 eggs	1 teaspoon baking soda
2 cups granulated sugar	1 teaspoon baking powder
1 cup oil	1/2 teaspoon salt
2 cups grated zucchini, packed tight	1 teaspoon ginger
1 teaspoon vanilla	1 teaspoon cinnamon
3 cups flour	1/2 teaspoon ground cloves
	1 cup walnuts, chopped

Preheat oven to 325°F. Combine eggs, sugar and oil. Add zucchini and vanilla, mix well. Sift together, flour, baking soda, baking powder, salt, ginger, cinnamon and cloves. Add to egg mixture slowly, using a mixer until blended well. Add walnuts and pour into greased 5 x 8 inch loaf pans. Bake for 1 hour. Cool for 1/2 hour before removing from pans.

DESSERTS
YAM FLAN TO PRICKLY PEAR SORBET

N ow we come to the best part of any meal, the dessert! Not only do I have Southwestern versions of traditional American desserts like *Dee Linda's Cherry Cobbler* (page 105) and *Chaco Chocolate Cake* (page 105), I have included desserts with a uniquely Southwestern flavor, such as *Apple Chili Pie* (page 104) and *Yam Flan* (page 102). I am sure the following recipes will touch your sweet tooth in one way or another.

❖ ——————————————— ❖ ——————————————— ❖

SANTA FE HORNS

This lovely dessert is turning up in many Southwestern restaurants.

INGREDIENTS FOR CRUST:

1 cup sugar   1/4 cup water
3/4 cup blanched almonds

INGREDIENTS FOR FILLING:

Vanilla ice cream   1 pint raspberries
Mandarin orange slices   1 pint blackberries

INGREDIENTS FOR SAUCE:

2 cups milk   4 egg yolks, beaten
1/2 cup sugar   1 teaspoon vanilla
1/4 cup flour

Preheat oven to 375°F. Grind sugar and almonds in a blender until very fine. Add water and blend until mixture becomes a paste. Let sit for 10 minutes. Place parchment paper over cookie sheet and spoon 1 inch balls of dough, leaving 4 inches in between each cookie. Bake in top half of oven for about 12 minutes, until evenly browned. Use scissors to cut paper between cookies and quickly fold edges of the paper, pulling each cookie into a horn shape. Let cool. Work quickly because once cookies cool they cannot be reshaped. To prepare custard sauce; scald milk and set aside. Using the top of a double boiler over hot water, blend sugar, flour and egg yolks. Mix well. Add scalded milk very slowly. Blend well. Cook, stirring constantly, until it begins to boil and can coat a spoon. Remove from heat and add vanilla. Stir well. Once cookies have cooled, fill with softened vanilla ice cream. Spoon vanilla sauce around filled cookie and add fruit. Makes 8 horns.

Santa Fe Horn

NANNA'S APRICOT PIE

My grandmother, Mary V. Barker, who we lovingly called Nanna, was the only person I know who ever made apricot pies using dried apricots. This is a Hilburn tradition that has been carried on by my sister, Dee Linda. The custard sauce is a new addition.

INGREDIENTS FOR CRUST:

2 cups sifted flour
1 teaspoon salt
2/3 cup shortening

4 teaspoons butter
1/2 cup ice water

INGREDIENTS FOR FILLING:

2 bags dried apricots
3 cups sugar
1/2 teaspoon nutmeg

1/2 teaspoon cinnamon
Water

INGREDIENTS FOR CUSTARD SAUCE:

6 egg yolks
2 cups heavy cream
1/2 cup sugar
2 teaspoons cornstarch

2 cups half and half
2 teaspoons vanilla extract
3 ounces white chocolate

To prepare crust; combine flour and salt, add shortening and butter, cutting into flour with a knife. When mixture consists of pebble sized lumps add ice water, a little at a time, until dough forms a ball. Cover with plastic and chill for 1/2 hour. Roll dough on a lightly floured board. Preheat oven to 425°F. To prepare filling; place apricots in a medium saucepan and cover with water. Bring to a boil and add sugar. Simmer until apricots are tender, but not mushy. Add nutmeg and cinnamon. Pour filling into uncooked pie crust and cover with top crust, pricking with a fork in an attractive design to allow steam to vent. To prepare sauce; mix egg yolks with the cornstarch, sugar and 1 1/2 cups heavy cream. In a small saucepan bring half and half to a boil. Cook over very low heat for 5 minutes. Set aside. Using a double boiler, heat 1/2 cup cream in the top pan and add white chocolate. When the chocolate melts, whisk until smooth. Keep warm. Stir 1/2 cup hot cream into egg yolk mixture then gently stir egg yolks into remaining hot cream. Add white chocolate cream to mixture. Stir and cook over low heat until custard thickens, approximately 4 minutes. When mixture coats the back of a spoon, strain into a bowl. To serve; pour custard sauce on a dessert plate and place a piece of Nanna's Apricot Pie on top of sauce.

LEMON-PINEAPPLE MOUSSE

Here is a light and tasty sweet that is low in fat but high in flavor.
Serve as a snack or a light dessert.

INGREDIENTS:

1 box lemon gelatin	1 1/2 tablespoons lemon juice
2 cups boiling water	3 tablespoons lemon rind, grated
1 pint pineapple sherbet	

Mix gelatin into boiling water. Add sherbet, lemon juice and 1 tablespoon
lemon rind. Using an electric mixer, beat on low until sherbet melts.
Pour into 6 dessert dishes and chill until set. Garnish with remaining
lemon rind. Serves 6.

SQUASH PIE

The spices in this pie give it the rich, sweet flavor of the Southwest.
Garnish with a lovely hibiscus blossom to add a touch of elegance.

INGREDIENTS:

1 pound yellow squash	1/2 teaspoon allspice
1/4 cup honey	2 teaspoons cinnamon
1 tablespoon molasses	2 eggs
1/4 teaspoon ginger	

Preheat oven to 325° F. Steam squash until it becomes tender. Cool
before cutting in half. Place both halves in blender with honey, molasses,
ginger, allspice, cinnamon and eggs. Blend well. Turn into large baking
pan (more than one may be needed). Bake for 1 hour. Serves 12.

PRICKLY PEAR SORBET

INGREDIENTS:

8 prickly pear fruit, peeled	Juice from 1/2 lemon
6 tablespoons sugar	

In a blender, blend fruit then strain. Add sugar and lemon juice and place
in an ice cream maker. Follow manufacturer's instructions to make ice
cream. Garnish with a sprig of mint. Serves 4.

YAM FLAN

This is a Southwestern version of the more traditional Mexican Flan, a yummy creation that is both colorful and tastes divine.

INGREDIENTS:

1 1/2 pounds yams	1 cup half and half
1 1/2 cups sugar	1 cup heavy cream
3/4 cup water	1 1/4 teaspoons vanilla
8 eggs	1/2 teaspoon cinnamon
2 egg yolks	1/2 teaspoon nutmeg
1 14 ounce can sweetened	1/2 teaspoon allspice
condensed milk	

Clean yams and bake at 325° F for about 1 1/2 hours. When yams have been cooked until soft, peel and purée. There should be 1 1/2 cups puréed yams. Set aside. Prepare caramel by bringing sugar and 1/4 cup water to a boil in a large saucepan. Do not stir. When syrup becomes lightly brown and bubbles, pour syrup into a 9 inch glass flan pan or dish, turning dish until syrup covers the entire bottom and some of the sides. Pour excess syrup back into pot and add remaining 1/2 cup water and bring to a boil. This thinner syrup will be served with flan. Set aside. Combine eggs and egg yolks and beat until fluffy. Add condensed milk, half and half, vanilla, cinnamon, nutmeg, allspice and puréed yams and beat well. Pour mixture into the prepared dish and set inside a roasting pan. Pour boiling water into roasting pan until water comes half way up side of flan dish. Bake until flan is firm, about 1 hour. Take flan dish out of water and cool to room temperature before refrigerating. Remove flan by sliding a moistened knife around edge of dish. Place serving plate over top of flan and flip over, flan should slide out easily. Serve with remaining syrup.

❖―――――――――❖―――――――――❖

GRANOLA BARS

INGREDIENTS:

1/2 cup butter	1/2 cup coconut
2/3 cup peanut butter	1/2 cup Grapenut Cereal
1/3 cup honey	2 1/2 cups oatmeal

Preheat oven to 350°F. Combine butter, peanut butter and honey in a saucepan. Cook over very low heat until melted. Add coconut, Grapenut Cereal and oatmeal. Mix well and turn into a glass baking dish. Bake for 18 minutes and cut into squares. Cool before serving.

Prickly Pear Sorbet and Lemon Ice

PICACHO PEAK PINEAPPLE PLEASURE

Picacho Peak, 45 miles northwest of Tucson, was the site of the western most battle of the civil war. There may be a civil war at your house over who gets the last piece!

INGREDIENTS:

1 large pineapple	1 tablespoon packed brown sugar
2/3 cup sour cream	1/2 cup pecans, chopped
2 tablespoons sugar	

Slice 1/3 off the side of a pineapple, leaving the crown. Use a grapefruit knife to remove fruit to 1/2 inch of shell. Remove fruit, discarding core, and cut into bite sized pieces. Sprinkle sugar over pineapple pieces and return to the pineapple shell. Mix sour cream and brown sugar and spoon over pineapple. Garnish with chopped pecans and serve. Serves 6.

❖━━━━━━━━━━━━❖━━━━━━━━━━━━❖

APPLE-CHILI PIE

This recipe combines the all-American dessert with the flavor of the Southwest. Experiment with the recipe and add more chili powder if you are brave enough, or like to live dangerously.

INGREDIENTS:

5 cups apples	1/2 teaspoon nutmeg
3 tablespoons butter	1 teaspoon chili powder
1 cup water	Salt
1 cup sugar	Pie crust (see recipe page 100)
1 teaspoon cinnamon	

Prepare pie crust ahead. Preheat oven to 375° F. Peel and slice apples. Place apples, water, sugar, cinnamon, nutmeg, chili powder and a dash of salt in a large saucepan. Cook over medium heat for 25 minutes. Pour apple mixture into prepared, uncooked pie crust and top with butter. Top with crust, prick vents into top of the crust using a fork and bake for 35 minutes, top crust should be golden brown.

❖━━━━━━━━━━━━❖━━━━━━━━━━━━❖

A WORD ABOUT SPICES:

Nutmeg, is the oval shaped, dried seed of an evergreen tree with a fruit similar to an apricot. Nutmeg has a sweet and spicy flavor and is often used to season meats and sauces also, cookies, pies and other pastries.

CHACO CHOCOLATE CAKE

I'm not sure if the Chaco Culture Indians of New Mexico really had a recipe like this, if they had, they might still be around today!

INGREDIENTS FOR CAKE:

1/2 cup butter, softened	1 cup sour milk
1 1/2 cups sugar	3 squares Hershey's Baking
2 eggs	Chocolate, melted
2 cups flour, sifted	1 teaspoon baking soda
1/2 teaspoon salt	1 tablespoon vinegar

INGREDIENTS FOR FROSTING:

3/4 cup butter, softened	1/2 teaspoon vanilla
3 cups powdered sugar	1/4 cup milk
1/2 cup cocoa	

To prepare the cake: preheat oven to 375° F. Combine sugar and butter, creaming them together. Add 1 egg and beat well. Add remaining egg and beat well. Stir in flour and salt add, alternately, with milk, beating well. Dissolve baking soda in vinegar and add to cake mixture with melted chocolate, mixing well. Grease 9-inch cake pans and pour cake mixture into pans. Bake for 25 minutes and set aside to cool. To prepare frosting; cream butter with one cup sugar. Add remaining sugar, cocoa, vanilla and milk. Beat until smooth. When cake has completely cooled, spread frosting over top of the bottom layer before topping with second layer of cake. Finish cake by frosting top and sides. Serves 8.

DEE LINDA'S CHERRY COBBLER

Once again, my sister Dee Linda offers one of her wonderful recipes. It's easy to make and can be served with ice-cream or whipped cream.

INGREDIENTS:

1 cup uncooked oatmeal	1 cup brown sugar, firmly packed
1 cup flour	1/2 cup butter
1/4 teaspoon salt	1 21 ounce can cherry pie filling

Preheat oven to 350° F. Mix oatmeal, flour, salt and brown sugar. Cut in butter until crumbly. Place half of the mixture into a well greased 8 x 8 inch pan. Layer with pie filling and spread remaining oat mixture over cherry filling. Bake for 45 minutes and serve hot.

PUMPKIN SQUARES

Here is a new twist to an American tradition. The pecan topping gives it an extra sweet touch.

INGREDIENTS FOR CRUST:

1/2 cup oatmeal   1/2 cup butter, melted
1 cup flour   1/2 cup brown sugar

INGREDIENTS FOR FILLING:

1 16 ounce can pumpkin   2 eggs
1 large can evaporated milk   1 1/2 teaspoons cinnamon
3/4 cup sugar   1/4 teaspoon ground cloves

INGREDIENTS FOR TOPPING:

2 tablespoons butter, softened   1/2 cup brown sugar
1/2 cup chopped pecans

To prepare crust; preheat oven to 350° F. Combine oatmeal, flour, butter and brown sugar. Press into a 9x13 inch pan. Bake for 15 minutes. To prepare filling; combine pumpkin, evaporated milk, sugar, eggs, cloves and cinnamon. Mix well and pour into baked crust. Bake for 20 minutes. To prepare topping; mix pecans, brown sugar and butter. Sprinkle over top of pie. Bake for 20 more minutes. Cool before cutting into squares.

❖————————————————❖————————————————❖

BAKED APPLES

This simple dessert is the perfect ending to any meal. Top with whipped cream or ice cream.

INGREDIENTS:

4 large Golden Delicious or Rome   4 teaspoons butter
Beauty apples, unpared   1/2 teaspoon ground cinnamon
3 tablespoons brown sugar   Water

Preheat oven to 375°F. Core apples and pare a 1 inch strip around the middle of each apple. Place apples in a baking dish and place 2 teaspoons sugar, 1 teaspoon butter and a dash of cinnamon in the center of each apple. Sprinkle tops with cinnamon. Add 1/4 inch water to baking dish. Bake for 30 to 40 minutes, until apples are tender when pierced with a fork. Baste with syrup during baking. Serves 4.

CRÉME BRULÉE

Many of the better restaurants here in the Southwest offer this elegant creation on their dessert menus.

INGREDIENTS:

2 cups heavy cream	4 egg yolks
1 vanilla bean, split	5 tablespoons sugar

Preheat oven to 325° F. In the top of a double boiler, pour cream and add vanilla bean. Cover and cook over boiling water until a wrinkled skin develops over surface, scalding point. In a separate bowl, beat egg yolks and 1 tablespoon sugar until light in color. Remove vanilla bean from cream and pour cream into egg yolk mixture very slowly, stirring constantly. Return mixture to pan and cook over boiling water, stirring constantly, until custard thickens enough to coat a wooden spoon. Make sure the mixture never comes to a boil, or it will curdle. Strain custard into a shallow baking dish and bake for 5 to 8 minutes. When skin forms on top, remove from oven and refrigerate for 3 to 4 hours, or overnight. Preheat broiler. Sprinkle top of cold crème with 4 tablespoons sugar and place under a heated broiler, 4 inches from broiler. Make sure broiler is very hot to prevent custard from bubbling through sugar topping. If this starts to happen, remove dish at once or custard will burn. When crème is complete, refrigerate for 2 to 3 hours before serving. Serves 6.

❖━━━━━━━━━━━━━❖━━━━━━━━━━━━━❖

OATMEAL AND ALMOND COOKIES

INGREDIENTS:

1/2 cup sugar	1/2 cup toasted almonds, ground
1/2 cup brown sugar, packed	
1/2 cup butter, softened	1/2 teaspoon baking soda
1/2 teaspoon vanilla	1/4 teaspoon baking powder
1 large egg	1/8 teaspoon salt
1 1/2 cups fast cooking oats	1/2 cup almonds, sliced
1/2 cup flour	

Preheat oven to 375°F. Combine sugar, brown sugar, butter, vanilla and egg. Mix well. Add oats, flour, ground almonds, baking soda, baking powder and salt, mixing well. Add sliced almonds. Place rounded teaspoonfuls of dough onan ungreased cookie sheet, about 2 inches apart. Bake for 10 minutes, or until golden brown. Cool before removing from cookie sheet. Makes about 36 cookies.

LEMON ICE

Here is another light and cool dessert that is just the perfect thing to serve at a barbeque, or when your family is out by the pool.

INGREDIENTS:

3/4 cup lemon juice, fresh is best
3 1/2 cups water
1 1/2 cups sugar

2 tablespoons lemon zest
1 lemon, sliced thin

Bring water to a boil in a saucepan and add sugar, stirring until dissolved. Remove from heat and let cool. Add lemon juice and zest. When lemon mixture has cooled, pour into an ice cream maker and follow the manufacturers instructions for making ice cream. Garnish with lemon slices and serve in decorative ice cream dishes, or in cocktail glasses. Serves 6.

❖ ———————————— ❖ ———————————— ❖

BAKED PEACHES

Place baked peaches in an attractive bowl for an elegant presentation.

INGREDIENTS:

4 large ripe peaches
1 pound apricots, pitted
2 cups water
1 1/4 cups fine sugar

1/4 cup brown sugar, packed
1/2 cup chopped pecans
1/2 cup coconut
2 tablespoons butter, softened

Combine apricots, water and 1 cup fine sugar in saucepan. Bring mixture to a boil and simmer for 7 minutes. Set aside. Blanch peaches in boiling water for 2 minutes. Dip peaches in ice water which will make removal of the skin very easy. Cut off the top of the peach at the pit. Remove pit. Combine brown sugar, pecans, coconut and 1 tablespoon butter. Fill peaches with pecan mixture. Grease a baking pan with the remaining butter and place peaches on pan with apricots surrounding them. Discard poaching fluid. Top with remaining sugar and bake for 8 to 10 minutes. Remove peaches to serving dishes then place baking pan on the stove over medium heat to reduce juices. Purée apricots in a blender and push purée through a sieve. Spoon the apricot sauce around the peaches and serve. Serves 4.

❖ ———————————— ❖ ———————————— ❖

A WORD ABOUT SPICES:

Spices are aromatic by-products of dried seeds, buds, bark, parts of flowers and roots of plants. They are most often of tropical origin.

CHEESECAKE

The simplicity of a basic cheesecake is one of the joys of life. No cookbook is complete without a good cheesecake recipe.

INGREDIENTS FOR CRUST:

2 1/2 cups graham cracker crumbs

3/4 cup butter, melted

INGREDIENTS FOR FILLING:

1 8 ounce package cream cheese, softened
1/2 cup sugar
1 tablespoon lemon juice

1/2 teaspoon vanilla
2 eggs
Salt

INGREDIENTS FOR TOPPING:

1 1/2 cups sour cream
3 tablespoons sugar

3/4 teaspoon vanilla

To prepare crust; combine cracker crumbs and butter and press into a 9 inch buttered pie plate, building up the sides. Preheat oven to 325°F. To prepare the filling; beat cream cheese until fluffy. Blend in sugar, lemon juice, vanilla, and salt. Add eggs, one at a time, beating after each. Pour filling into crust and bake for 25 to 30 minutes, until set.For the topping; combine sour cream, sugar and vanilla and spread over top of hot cheese cake. Bake for 10 more minutes. Chill before serving.

RICE PUDDING

Rice pudding is enjoyed by children everywhere. How long has it been since you've had this dessert?

INGREDIENTS:

2 cups cooked rice
3 cups milk
1/4 cup brown sugar
1 cup raisins

1/4 teaspoon cinnamon
1/4 teaspoon nutmeg
3 eggs, beaten

Preheat oven to 325° F. Combine beaten eggs, rice, milk, sugar, raisins, cinnamon and nutmeg. Mix well. Pour into a greased casserole dish. Bake for about one hour, or until set. Serve hot or cold. Serves 6.

BANANA FRITTERS

INGREDIENTS:

1 egg, separated	2 teaspoons butter, melted
1/3 cup milk	4 bananas, peeled
1/2 cup flour	Juice of one lemon
2 teaspoons sugar	2 tablespoons powdered sugar
1/2 teaspoon baking powder	Vegetable oil
1/2 teaspoon salt	Whipped Cream

Beat egg white stiff. Beat the yolk and add milk. Combine flour, sugar, baking powder and salt and add to beaten egg yolk. Add melted butter and fold in egg white. Cut bananas into 2 inch chunks and dip in lemon juice. Sprinkle bananas with powdered sugar then dip chunks into the batter. Fry in 2 inches of hot oil. Top with whipped cream and serve hot.

❖────────────────❖────────────────❖

DESSERT TAMALES

INGREDIENTS:

3 1/2 dozen dry corn husks	1 cup brown sugar
4 cups masa harina flour	1/2 teaspoon cinnamon
1 cup lard	1/4 cup butter
1 cup sugar	1 cup pitted dates, chopped
1 teaspoon salt	1 cup pecans, chopped

In a large saucepan, cover corn husks with boiling water. Soak for at least 30 minutes. Beat lard until fluffy, using mixer. Combine masa flour, sugar and salt. Gradually add the flour and sugar mixture to lard and add water until dough sticks together and has a pastelike consistency. To prepare date filling; blend the brown sugar, butter and cinnamon until smooth. Dry husks by placing on paper towels and patting dry. Add chopped dates and pecans and mix evenly. Spread 2 tablespoons tamale dough on center portion of husk, leaving at least a 2 inch margin at both ends and about a 1/2 inch margin on the right side. Spoon 1 1/2 table-spoons filling onto dough. Wrap tamale, overlapping left side first, then right side slightly over left. Fold bottom up and top down. Lay tamales in top section of steamer with open flaps on bottom. Tie with string if husks are too short to stay closed. Tamales may completely fill the top section of steamer but should be placed so there are spaces between them for the circulation of steam. Steam over simmering water for 1 hour, until corn husks can be peeled from dough easily. Makes 3 1/2 dozen.

BEVERAGES
FROM TEA TO TEQUILA

One of the basic tenets of Southwestern living is an emphasis on casual simplicity. This is reflected in many of the beverages served with foods of the Southwest. Tequila is the perfect example. Originally served in shot glasses, or straight from the bottle, with a wedge of lime and a shaker of salt on the side, until someone simplified things by combining the three, adding a dash of Triple Sec, and pouring it over ice. Variations of this drink, now called *Margaritas*, are being served all over America. The drinks in this chapter compliment the spicy foods served in the Southwest and help douse fires in the mouths of many chile lovers. Sample these drinks to discover which suits you best.

❖―――――――――❖―――――――――❖

MARGARITA

Legend has it that the Margarita was invented by a bartender in Tijuana, Mexico who named it after a beautiful Hollywood star.

INGREDIENTS:

4 ounces tequila (preferably Cuervo Gold)
2 tablespoons Triple Sec
1/4 cup lime juice

1 lime, sliced
1 1/2 teaspoons sugar
Salt
Crushed Ice

Combine tequila, Triple Sec, lime juice, sugar and crushed ice. Blend on high. Rub a lime slice around the rim of chilled glasses and dip in salt. Pour Margarita mixture into glasses and garnish with slices of lime.

❖―――――――――❖―――――――――❖

ORANGE SPRITZER

INGREDIENTS:

2 medium peaches
1 cup fresh orange juice
1/2 cup fresh lemon juice

2 tablespoons sugar
8 ice cubes
Orange slices

Rinse, slice and pit peaches. Place peaches, orange juice, lemon juice, sugar and ice in a blender and blend until smooth. Garnish with orange slices. Serve in tall glasses.

PINEAPPLE PLEASURE

This pineapple drink is exactly the right thing to serve on those hot summer days when everyone is spending time around the pool.

INGREDIENTS:

1/2 cup canned or fresh crushed
pineapple with juice, frozen
3/4 cup milk (nonfat or regular)
1/4 teaspoon rum flavoring

1/8 teaspoon nutmeg
1/8 teaspoon cinnamon
2 teaspoons sugar

Place frozen crushed pineapple, milk, rum flavoring, nutmeg, cinnamon and sugar in a blender. Blend on high until creamy. Pour into chilled glasses and serve. Serves 2.

SANGRITA

Sangritas are the perfect chaser to a shot of Tequila. The spicy flavor enhances the flavor of tequila and lightens its burning sensation.

INGREDIENTS:

1/2 cup orange juice
2 cups chilled tomato juice
2 jalapeño peppers, seeded and
diced
1/4 cup onion, minced

1 tablespoon lime juice
2 teaspoons sugar
1/2 teaspoon hot pepper sauce
1/2 teaspoon salt

Combine orange juice, tomato juice, jalapeño peppers, onion, lime juice, sugar, hot pepper sauce and salt in a blender. Blend until smooth. Chill before serving. Serves 4.

ICED COFFEE

INGREDIENTS:

Pot of your favorite coffee
Ice cubes

Sugar
Cream

Make a pot of your favorite coffee and pour into tall glasses over ice. Add sugar and cream to taste. Serves 4 to 6.

MEXICAN PUNCH

This is a fresh and zesty cooler perfect for any fiesta or pool party. Serve whenever your favorite friends gather together.

INGREDIENTS:

2 ounces cranberry juice
2 ounces grenadine
2 ounces piña colada mix

2 ounces pineapple juice
Splash of 7-Up
Ice

Place cranberry juice, grenadine, piña colada mix and pineapple juice in a blender. Blend and pour into tall glasses over ice. Add splash of 7-Up and garnish with orange slices if desired. Serves 2.

TEQUILA SUNRISE

The Tequila Sunrise is as well known as the Margarita. Both symbolize the low-key atmosphere of the Southwest.

INGREDIENTS:

4 ounces tequila (preferably Cuervo Gold)
1 cup fresh orange juice
2 teaspoons lime juice

2 tablespoons grenadine
Crushed Ice
Maraschino Cherries

Combine tequila, orange juice, lime juice and grenadine in a blender or shaker. Pour into tall glasses over ice. Garnish with a cherry. Serves 2.

KILLER CRANBERRY COCKTAIL

INGREDIENTS:

4 ounces cranberry juice
1/2 ounce Cranberry Schnapps
1 ounce vodka

6 cubes of ice
Lime slices

Combine cranberry juice, cranberry Schnapps, vodka and ice in blender. Blend until smooth. Pour into chilled glasses and garnish with lime slices.

SANGRIA

This red wine punch is a traditional favorite from Mexico that crossed the border to be enjoyed by many in the Southwest.

INGREDIENTS:

1 bottle red wine	1 orange, sliced
1 cup orange juice	2 cups fresh pineapple, cubed
1 7 ounce bottle club soda	Ice, cubes or chopped
1 lime, sliced	

Combine wine, orange juice, lime slices, orange slices and pineapple cubes and chill. Add club soda before serving. Pour over ice. Serves 6.

STRAWBERRY SPRITZER

Fresh strawberries are abundant in the Southwest. This combines fresh and frozen fruit to make a refreshing beverage.

INGREDIENTS:

1 pint fresh strawberries	28 ounces carbonated water
3 10 ounce packages frozen strawberries	6 cups white grape juice

Thaw strawberries. Blend 2 packages of strawberries, with juice, until smooth. Pour into large punch bowl and add remaining package, with juice. Add grape juice and carbonated water, stir gently. Garnish with fresh strawberries.

MIMOSA

A wonderfully refreshing drink at any time, especially popular at brunch.

INGREDIENTS:

Fresh orange juice	Orange Slices
Champagne	

Pour orange juice and add Champagne to taste. Garnish with orange slices or fresh strawberries.

LEMON MIRAGE

Long time residents of the Southwest claim this drink helps make the summer heat a little easier to live with.

INGREDIENTS:

1 6 ounce can frozen lemonade	1 quart 7-Up, cold
1 6 ounce can frozen limeade	1 quart lemon/lime seltzer
1 6 ounce can frozen orange juice	Lemon slices
3 to 4 cups cold water	Orange slices

In a large punch bowl combine lemonade, limeade, orange juice, water, seltzer and 7-Up. Add lemon and orange slices. Serves 12

❖ ———————————————— ❖ ———————————————— ❖

HARD CIDER PUNCH

An excellent selection for entertaining on cool desert evenings, or during the festive holiday season.

INGREDIENTS:

2 quarts hard cider	2 tablespoons sugar
6 tablespoons brandy	2 oranges, stuck with 6 cloves
2 apples, sliced	each

In a large saucepan, combine cider, brandy, apples, sugar and cloved oranges. Simmer over medium to low heat for 25 minutes. Cool before serving from punch bowl. Serves 10.

❖ ———————————————— ❖ ———————————————— ❖

SUN TEA

Arizona boasts over 300 sunny days a year, and that means Sun Tea can be made almost every day in the Grand Canyon State.

INGREDIENTS:

1 gallon water	8 single tea bags

Find a gallon jug or jar and clean thoroughly. Fill with water and add tea bags. Cover and place in a sunny spot. When water becomes clear brown, bring indoors. To avoid clouding, let tea cool to room temperature before refrigerating. Pour over ice and add desired sweetener or lemon. For flavored teas, use flavored tea bags. Serves many!

INDEX

PHOTOGRAPHY PAGES 4, 5, 9, 13, 17, 25, 32, 33, 45, 51, 55, 58, 59, 70, 71, 73, 81, 85, 88, 99, 103 © RICHARD EMBERY. PHOTOGRAPHY PAGES 20, 21, 41, 67 © CAMELBACK DESIGN GROUP, INC.